JAPAN

Text by
ADOLFO TAMBURELLO

Foreword by
YASUNARI KAWABATA

MONUMENTS OF CIVILIZATION

JAPAN

MADISON SQUARE PRESS ®
GROSSET & DUNLAP

A National General Company

Publishers   New York

Frontispiece:
The series of roofs on the thirteen-story
pagoda of the Tanzan sanctuary. A.D. 1532
(Muromachi Period). Prefecture of Nara.

For permission to quote excerpts from the works indicated, we gratefully acknowledge the following:

W. N. Porter, *The Miscellany of a Japanese Priest* (Oxford Library of Prose and Poetry), 1914, London, Oxford University Press.

Omori, *Diaries of Court Ladies of Old Japan*, 1920, Houghton Mifflin Company.

Geoffrey Bownas and Anthony Thwaite (trs.), *The Penguin Book of Japanese Verse.* Copyright © Geoffrey Bownas and Anthony Thwaite, 1964. Penguin Books Ltd.

A. L. Sadler, *The Ten Foot Square Hut and Tales of the Heike*, 1928, Sydney, Australia, Angus and Robertson (Publishers). Courtesy of the estate of Professor A. L. Sadler.

W. G. Aston, *Nihongi — Chronicles of Japan from the Earliest Times to A.D. 697*, 1956, George Allen & Unwin Ltd. Courtesy of Paragon Book Reprint Corporation, New York City.

Post Wheeler, *The Sacred Scriptures of the Japanese*, published by Abelard-Schuman Ltd. in 1952. By Permission of Murnat Publications Inc.

Donald Keene, *Japanese Literature: An Introduction for Western Readers*, 1953, John Murray (Publishers) Ltd.

Makoto Ueda, *Literary and Art Theories in Japan*, Copyright © 1967 by The Press of Western Reserve University. Reprinted by permission of The Press of Western Reserve University, Cleveland, Ohio.

R. Tsunoda, Wm. Th. DeBary, Donald Keene (eds.), *Sources of Japanese Tradition*, 1958, Columbia University Press, New York City.

Basil Hall Chamberlain (trans.), *Ko-ji-ki, or Records of Ancient Matters*, II Edition, with notes by Aston. Published for the Asiatic Society of Japan by J. L. Thompson & Co., Kobe, Japan. 1932.

J. B. Snellen (trans.), *Nihongi*, from *Transactions of the Asiatic Society of Japan*, Vol. XIV, second series.

R. Tsunoda (trans.), *Japan in the Chinese Dynastic Histories.* Published by P. D. and Ione Perkins, Pasadena, California.

Basil Hall Chamberlain, *Things Japanese*, 3rd edition revised, 1898. John Murray (Publishers) Ltd., London.

A MADISON SQUARE PRESS BOOK ®

First published in the United States in 1973
by Grosset & Dunlap, 51 Madison Avenue, New York 10010.

English translation copyright © 1973 by Mondadori, Milano-Kodansha,
Toyko: originally published in Italian under the title "*Grandi
Monumenti: Giappone*," copyright © 1971 by Mondadori, Milano-Kodansha,
Tokyo; copyright © 1971 by Kodansha Ltd., Tokyo, for the
illustrations; copyright © 1971 by Mondadori, Milano-Kodansha,
Tokyo, for the text.

First Printing

Editorial Director
GIULIANA NANNICINI

American Editorial Supervisor
JOHN BOWMAN

CONTENTS

FOREWORD

I once asked an Italian student of Japanese literature who was living in our country what had impressed him most about Japan. "The abundance of green," he immediately replied. His words made me think again of my country's verdure, so much more abundant than in Italy, perhaps more abundant than in any Western nation. Japanese vegetation is less luminous than the European or the Southern variety; it is paler and more aqueous. Yet closer examination shows a color that in its wealth of nuance, in the delicacy of its infinite tonalities, is probably unique in the world. This can be viewed most clearly in the spring, when the leaves are newborn, or in the autumn, when the same leaves turn color again. Japan has perhaps a greater variety of trees and flowers than any country in the world, but Japan's beauty is not due to its wealth of flowers and trees alone. There are mountains with marvelous scenery, fascinating rivers and seas, and the exquisite and unusual variability of the seasons. The sensibility of the Japanese has always been conditioned by this climate, by this evocative natural environment. It has definitively affected all that we have built, and the art we have made.

The mausoleum of the Emperor Nintoku, for instance, built in the fifth century A.D., is larger than the Egyptian pyramids, yet it is no more than a hill surrounded by a moat and adorned with woods and lovely rows of trees. There is no architectural construction; everything is expressed by the trees. The group of ancient tombs in the Saitobaru area of the island of Kyushu is an agglomeration of hills. Both the seventh-century sanctuary of Ise, whose purity and simplicity have made it a typical example of Japanese taste to the West, and the seventeenth-century Toshogu temple of Nikko, as florid and gaudy a masterpiece of craftsmanship as can be imagined, are situated alike: on mountains, in the middle of a vast extent of woods, firmly in the midst of nature. The boundless landscape around these temples is itself the sacred area; one can almost say that the scenery itself is the temple. In ancient Japan, of course, this was literally true. The high mountains, the great forests, the falls, fountains, cliffs, stones — even the old trees — were considered divinities or images of the divine. The idea persists today in popular traditions. The cliffs of Futamiga-ura in the Bay of Ise and the falls of Nachi at Kumano are two examples of such natural features.

Related to this feeling for nature is the Japanese feeling for the associations of a place or of a structure. Both the Itsukushima temple at Miyajima, which seems almost to float on the Seto Sea, and the Hikari-do chapel in the Chusonji temple (the chapel of the lights), entirely covered with gold, were built in the twelfth century, in the period of transition between the imperial government of Heian and the Kamakura military regime. They show the penetration of the elegance prevalent in the capital, Kyoto, to the remote eastern and western regions of the country; yet they are loved by the people not so much for this as for their association with the *Heike Monogatari*, the thirteenth-century historical drama that describes the fall of the house of the Taira (Heike) and the death of Yoshitsune, their antagonist, one of the most romantic figures in Japanese history. Whoever visits the temples thinks of episodes from the epic or from the fifteenth-century *Gikei-ki*, the "Life of Yoshitsune." Such places, recalling legends, legendary feats, or historical facts, are called *utamakura* (poetic references) in Japanese, and they are celebrated by poems in traditional forms such as the *tanka* or the *haiku*. Pilgrimages to these places made by literary men are immortalized in their travel journals, and in some cases this literature has given life to its own *utamakura*, such as the spots described in the *Ise Monogatari*, the "Tales of Ise" of the fifteenth century, or the *Oku no Hosomichi*, "Paths to the North," by Basho, written in the late seventeenth century.

Almost all these places are immersed in nature, yet they are all evidence of the penetration of civilization into every corner of Japan. Nor has the tradition been broken in modern times. The recently built Palace of International Congresses, at Kyoto, lies on the shoulders of the ancient capital, surrounded by hills, in a delicate scene of noble elegance. Nevertheless, the edifices that have been placed in nature are immensely diverse. They range from works of such finesse and dexterity as the gold chapel of Hiraizumi and the Toshogu mausoleum at Nikko to the mystic simplicity of the stone garden of Ryoanji, or the buildings and the garden of the imperial villa at Katsura.

Western lovers of Japanese civilization prefer to take work of the latter sort — the mystic simplicity — as the norm; it is their way of interpreting our entire artistic tradition. Many Japanese feel the same way. *Noh* theater is preferred to *kabuki*, black ink painting to color painting, pottery in subdued colors from the kilns at Shino and Karatsu to the smooth surfaces and brilliant colors of the wares from Nabeshima and Imari, rough and harsh *tsumigi* silk to the soft, embroidered, multi-colored *yuzen* silk. It is difficult to deny that the more austere works represent a tendency in Japanese civilization. It has been evident from ancient times, and may perhaps be said to have reached its peak with the influx of Zen Buddhism and the growth of the spirit of the tea ceremony in the Middle Ages. Basho wrote: "The same spirit lies at the heart of Sesshu's painting, the *renga* poetry of Sogi, and the tea cult introduced by Rikyu." The statement is true, but it is disturbing. Sesshu (1420–1506) brought rough-brush, black ink drawing to its perfection, Sogi (1421–1502) was the master of *renga* poetry, and Rikyu (1521–1591) of the tea cult. And *haiku* poetry reached its peak in the seventeenth century, with Basho's work. Yet there are great, and very different, works of Japanese civilization much earlier in time. The "Tale of Genji," written at the beginning of the eleventh century, is a novel that still has no rival in all Japanese literature, and *waka* poetry is best represented in the eighth-century anthology *Manyoshu*, the tenth-century anthology *Kokinshu*, and the thirteenth-century anthology *Skin Kokinshu*.

The greatest Japanese sculpture was done in the Asuka and Tenpyo periods, from the sixth century to the middle of the eighth; religious painting, jewelry, and goldwork flourished in the Heian period, which lasted from the end of the eighth century to the end of the twelfth. The Horyuji temple, a jewel of sacred architecture and the oldest extant wood construction in the world, was built in the seventh century. Nor are these the oldest works of value. The marvelous terra-cotta figures called *haniwa* come from the Yayoi period, which lasted from the third or second century B.C. to the second or third century A.D. They are full of delicacy, innocence, and refined simplicity. Earlier than the *haniwa* are the vases and figurines of the Jomon civilization, so virile and violent in form that at times they touch upon the monstrous.

Periods of roughness seem to alternate with periods of delicacy in Japanese civilization. The shift from Jomon to Yayoi might be compared to the transition from the virile Nara civilization to the delicacy of the Heian age. It is difficult to generalize about such variety. Besides the phases already mentioned, Japanese history includes the vigorous Kamakura era, the reserved Muromachi, the graceful and gay Momoyama and Genroku periods, not to mention the modern era. Yet the art of Japan in all ages contains a spirit not unrelated to the quality of landscape I spoke of earlier. It is the spirit the Japanese call *mono no aware*, which could be defined as the search for contemplative harmony, carried on in the knowledge that everything in the world, and the world itself, is mortal and must pass. In Japanese aesthetics, *mono no aware* is a constant and abiding presence.

YASUNARI KAWABATA
(1899-1972)

INTRODUCTION

Japanese culture is by now rather well-known in the West. Some aspects of it, such as *judo, ikebana* (flower arrangement), the tea ceremony, and *Zen*, have fascinated the Western public for quite some time. Although these are certainly not the least valid aspects of Japanese civilization, they are without a doubt the most easily misunderstood. Vague spiritual needs may justify the mistaken interpretations that often result, but all too many people are thus led to believe that they can find in the Japanese world, and in a spirituality of a supposedly pure Eastern type, a panacea for the crises and vacuums of today's mechanical Western civilization. Yet the spiritual values to be found in the Oriental civilizations are neither more nor less vital than those of the West. At the basis of the belief that salvation lies in the Orient is the ingenuous faith or the tacit hope that Eastern culture has been wholly preserved in its purity, immune from the contaminations of the modern world. Perhaps this is because so much has been said — and wrongly — about Asiatic isolation.

With Japan, the idea of a supposedly total isolation has been reinforced by the fact that it is an island. This view has been authoritatively supported by scholars who, interpreting history in geographic terms, have considered insularity the same thing as isolation. But if it is true that for a long period Japanese political history remained detached from Western history, it is also true that from a very remote age Japan lived within the context of the great Asiatic, or better, Euro-Asiatic civilizations, and continued to live there even during periods of the most tenacious obscurantist or closed door policies. Indeed, Japanese culture has never had a really isolated, stagnant phase. It may seem surprising, for instance, that Japanese portrait painting shows many points of contact with the European variety, with Alexandrine and Roman portraiture particularly. Such similarities are neither fortuitous nor extraordinary. Classical art was imitated in many parts of Asia, partly because of the dynamics of its historical contacts and partly because of its suggestiveness; the most suitable climate and ground in Asia for the rebirth of those humanistic values that are the foundation of European civilization was found, at last, in Japan. It is fairly certain this is also the reason why Japan was able, with relative ease, to accept Western civilization in the last century, and to follow the path that has led to its becoming a great power in modern times.

Since it has been the custom to regard the archipelago as the Thule of Asia, or at best as a distant Chinese province, the cosmopolitan spirit and thrust of Japanese civilization have regularly failed to be noticed. The sea that separates the Japanese islands from the coasts of the continent has often been a barrier against massive invasions, but it has also been a communications link, connecting Japan with the numerous and diverse points on the Asiatic continent from which, over the centuries, its different ethnic and cultural elements have come. From the southern areas came the maritime tradition and agricultural civilization; from the northern areas came the traditions of the nomadic world, which have given a militaristic stamp to Japanese civilization. In this sense, the four large islands and the many smaller ones that make up the archipelago form a tapestry of all the Asiatic civilizations, from those of the so-called Australasian world to those of the Chinese and central-Asian world. In the course of time, the intensity and continuity of contacts opened the country to Buddhist India and to Christian Europe. But these are the high points of an essentially continuous, limitless dialogue.

Now that East and West desire to meet on some common ground, not so much of mutual understanding as of some discovery of mutual values, Japan represents a leading voice in the dialogue. This is not only because it has proved capable, as a nation, of fusing Western and Eastern varieties of civilization, but because the Japanese variety of Oriental civilization seems to hold within it many elements of objective validity for the entire modern world. There are risks, of course, in applying certain types of philosophical speculation indiscriminately to modern scientific research or thought; *Zen* and psychoanalysis, for instance, have both suffered by being judged equivalent to each other. The speculative risks aside, however, Japanese culture proposes a great variety of effective values to our contemporaries.

Within the scope of this book, there is the example of architecture. The modular and spatial concepts of Japanese architecture have come to be utilized by modern architects throughout the world. Avant-garde movements such as rationalism and structuralism owe a great deal to Japan, too, as do impressionism and symbolism, whether in literature or in the figurative arts. The transistor radio is offered by some critics as the industrial exemplar of what they consider the core of Japanese culture: a painstaking and detailed art of small scale, which is ultimately affected and useless. Yet such a prejudice is obsolete, not to say erroneous. Neither modern Japanese culture nor the culture of the Japanese past is that of a society of ants. The fact that Japan has challenged the sway of the monumental in art and life, preferring to find its values within carefully considered hypotheses of limited proportions, is perhaps a more important lesson for the West than it wishes to admit.

NOTE: The use of Japanese terms has been limited as much as possible, in order not to overburden the text. Where Japanese terms are introduced, the English equivalents will be found next to the Japanese words. In the names of religious edifices, the "ji," "in," and "dera" endings (as in Horyuji, Byodoin, Fukidera) indicate Buddhist temples. The "gu" ending and the words *jingu* and *taisha* indicate a Shinto sanctuary.

MAP OF THE JAPANESE PREFECTURES

*(Names of the ancient prefectures in Italics;
those of the present day in Roman type.)*

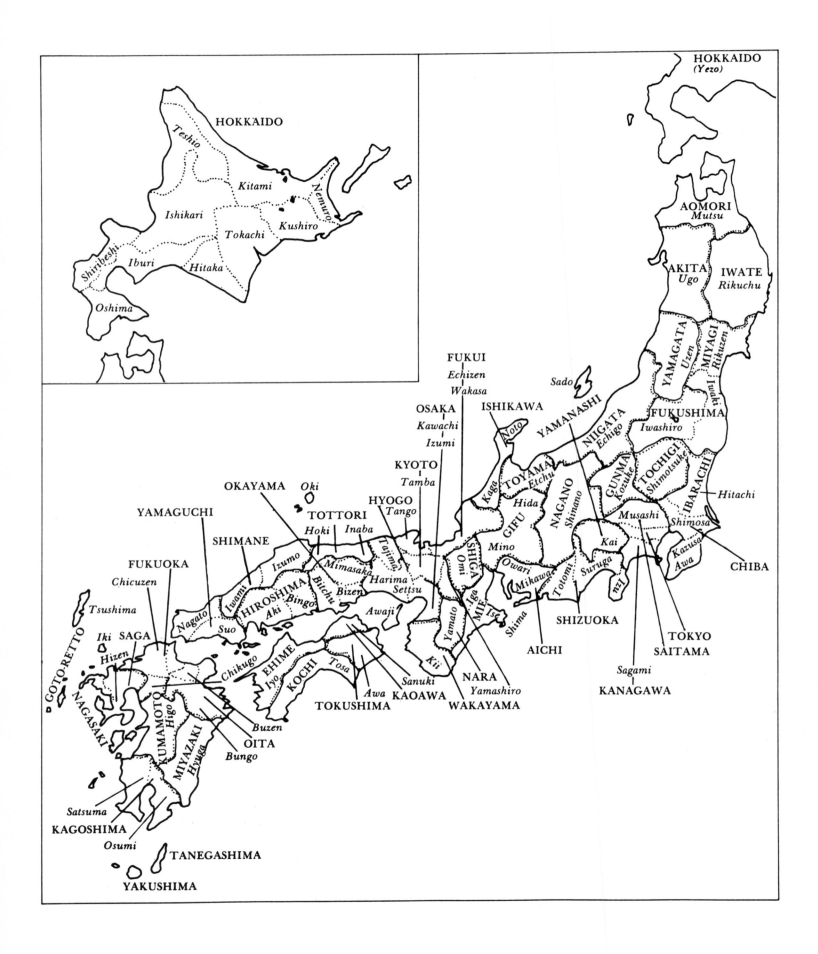

THE ORIGINS

The Stone Age

For a long time it was thought that Japan had first been populated only a few thousand years before Christ by Neolithic (New Stone Age) peoples, who came from the Asian continent by sea. Recently, however, a much more ancient settlement has been discovered. In the excavation of an area on the island of Kyushu in 1961, human fossils and handmade stone implements, dating back to very ancient examples brought to light in China and Indonesia, were discovered. The find confirmed fully the thesis of a *Nipponanthropus*, boldly set forth forty years ago on the basis of an enigmatic fossil finding and claiming that Japan was originally inhabited by palaeoanthropi not unlike the Java Pithecanthropus, or Peking Man, the Sinanthropus. Since the thesis of Japan Man was originally set out, geological research has verified that the present-day physical configuration of the archipelago is not particulrly old. As little as twenty, or even ten thousand years ago, the islands were an almost continuous stretch of land, connected to the Asian continent in many places; what is now the Japan Sea was a large lakelike basin. It is likely that many types of mammals moved into the country by means of land routes, to thrive in the pastures of Japan's interior; the influx included mammoths from the Siberian north and elephants from the south. The first hominoids to live in the country came across at the same terrestrial points, attracted by these animals and by the abundant wild game the land contained.

Japan was thus a converging point of migratory movements from both north and south. Cro-Magnon groups probably descended into the area from the north, bringing a relatively evolved Paleolithic culture, which flourished in the region for perhaps the last 100,000 years of the Ice Age. The distribution of findings from this group reveals a rather vast human expansion; the nature and disposition of the remains indicate that the people were hordes of hunters, living in refuges hidden in the dense forests and the underbrush. Unlike most of the early Stone Age settlements in the Euro-Asiatic regions, the primitive Japanese man had no great need for cave dwellings, but it appears that he soon acquired the capacity to build huts of branches or animal skins. Weapons and tools were originally large blocks of chipped stone; then the first spears and arrowheads appeared, becoming smaller and smaller until they were mostly of miniscule proportions. These so-called microliths characterize the Mesolithic, or intermediate, cultures of the end of the Ice Age and the post-Ice Age period, when the disappearance of the larger animals reduced the amount of quarry and the economy adapted itself to more modest hunting activities.

The outcome of these cultures is not known, but it was probably they who dealt with the pressures of the populations that brought the first Neolithic civilization to the archipelago. The recession of the glaciers and the rise of the sea level seems to have completely submerged the terrestrial passages sometime between 8,000 and 6,000

1. Neolithic terra-cotta statuette of a being with human and feral characteristics. Height 9.92 inches, width 8.07 inches. III–II millennium B.C. (Middle Jomon Period). From Kamikurogoma, Misaka-cho, Prefecture of Yamanashi. (Tokyo National Museum).

B.C., but Neolithic fishermen seem to have lost no time in reaching Japan by sea. Theirs was the Neolithic culture of northern Asia, particularly that of the protohistorical Siberian centers, and it is likely that they soon triumphed over the ancient hordes of the archipelago. The extreme coasts of Asia have always been an impassable bulwark for mass movements, however, so the Neolithic migration was probably not especially large. It had to overcome the difficulties of navigation in one of the most dangerous of sea basins.

The marked differences between the Neolithic cultures in each region of the archipelago over the course of time were due not only to local specialization but also to successive waves of migration, extended over many millennia, bringing diverse cultural traditions. There seems to have been no homogeneous ethnic type in Neolithic Japan. Recent discoveries have disproved the theory that the only Neolithic populations in the archipelago were the predecessors of the present-day Ainu, the proto-Caucasian population that still lives in the northern part of the country. According to the old theories, the Ainu first occupied the entire archipelago and were later pushed up to the north by Mongolian or north Asian races, who had migrated into Japan with their bronze and iron civilizations. Today it is thought that both the Ainu and the Japanese — that is to say, the predecessors of both populations — were present in the archipelago from the Neolithic Age onward, but that the Ainu, especially those who occupied the northern regions, were excluded from the process of assimilation that merged the other populations of the archipelago with the bearers of the metal cultures in the last centuries before Christ. The northern part of the country was completely cut off from historical Japanese culture, and Neolithic civilization lasted in certain areas up to the end of the first millennium of the Christian era. It was in the north that Neolithic civilization was first established, however, and it is not difficult to identify the Ainu as the heirs of the so-called paleo-European, proto-Caucasian populations, who settled on the Japanese coasts after long treks through northern Asia, before the southern areas underwent the Mongolian invasion.

Many elements in the ancient Neolithic Japanese world are linked with the economic and cultural world of northern Asia. The populations were not acquainted with agriculture, for instance. Like their contemporaries in north Asia they lived by fishing, hunting, and the gathering of uncultivated plants, continuing an economy typical of Mesolithic times. They lived a seminomadic existence, housed in half-buried hovels grouped together in villages. In the vicinity of these sites are massive deposits of shells, which eloquently reveal the principal nourishment of their populations. The habitations and the shell deposits are related to those of Siberian and Manchurian cultures. Similarities between the cultures extend to the bone and stone industries, as well as to pottery. This latter was made by hand without the use of the wheel and decorated with engraved motifs, often with the comblike ornament characteristic of the pottery art of Neolithic populations in northern Eurasia.

Although the origins of Japanese culture are indisputably northern, there were contributions from southern Asia as well, especially in the final Neolithic period, that is, the last three millennia before Christ. This is exemplified by the appearance of huts that, rather than being buried like the northern ones have their floors at ground level, and by the spread of a finished stone tool, the quadrangular ax, typical of agriculturally oriented Neolithic populations in the southeastern part of Asia. These contributions probably were followed by the introduction of agriculture and stock-raising in the archipelago, although there is little proof of this as yet. In any case, the Neolithic Japanese culture was a synthesis of elements diverse in their origins, which explains to some extent the ethnic and racial mixture that even now marks the country's population.

2. Neolithic terra-cotta vase with engraved and relief decorations in rope motifs. Height 23.42 inches, diameter of mouth 13.5 inches. III–II millennium B.C. (Middle Jomon Period). From Miyanomae, Ina, Prefecture of Nagano. (Tokyo National Museum).

Art of the Jomon

The regionalism typical of Japanese geography is another factor that impedes any study of the Neolithic culture as a unified complex. Over the period of several millennia the coastal populations remained completely differentiated from those of the mountains and the interior. The pottery attests to this. It varies greatly both in form and decoration, and is the most striking feature of the epoch. So undisputably does it characterize the Neolithic Japanese that he is usually called Jomon, from the type of rope decoration that dominated ceramics production for a long time. The whims of an inspired ornamental fantasy seem to have been satisfied by the production, during this period, of vast numbers of vases and statuettes. They are among the best and most refined examples of ceramic art in the protohistorical world. Besides signifying the imposing entrance of Japan into art history, the statuettes present a remarkable visual document of ideologies and symbols. The example in Figure 1, with its enigmatic figurative synthesis of the feral element with the human one, has given rise to innumerable hypotheses about the magic practices cultivated by populations who presumably believed in the demoniacal personification of animals. The vase in Figure 2 is a typical example of rope decoration, and dates back to the last phase of the Neolithic Age.

The fear of terrible metamorphoses, not only of men and animals but of the entire organic and inorganic world, has been preserved in Japanese tradition up to the present day. Most of the Jomon statuettes, however, have completely human characteristics. In some, human anatomy is given precedence; others are covered with a dense design that gives the idea of clothes, jewels, or even tattoos. A pronounced schematic pattern often reduces the upper limbs to mere stumps; the treatment of the face is rather summary, but at times has the virtue of a certain vivacity. In some specimens the head seems to be surmounted by large or heavy headdresses; in others the eyes occupy the entire head and are long cuts in oval-shaped frames.

In the search for some modern-day reference, these have been compared to the snow-glasses used by the populations of the extreme northern regions, and assumed to have been used also by the Neolithic Japanese. So strange in aspect are the sculptures that some critics have considered them depictions of extra-terrestrial beings, more than human, who at one point may have intervened in human history. Figure 3 evokes the curious image of a man in a diving-suit or overalls. The eyes, ears, and mouth are rendered graphically by little clay circles, in the characteristic figurative scheme of the heart-shaped motif that frames the face. The bust is dominated by a large central groove, which some have tried to explain by referring to the religious belief in a ventral line or life line. The notion of the venter, the belly, as an occult center of forces was very widespread in later Japanese philosophical speculation, but it is not known whether it is legitimate to project into such an ancient epoch the formulation of the idea. In this concept, *hara*, the belly, is considered the seat of primordial being, the receptacle of divinity and source of life energy. The later, sadly famous *hara-kiri* or *seppuku*, the cutting of the abdomen, derives from the notion; a form of suicide, it is practiced in order to strike directly at the vital center. Such an interpretation of these ancient sculptures is uncertain, however.

Much more reliable is the idea that the ventral line is related to sexual symbolism, faithful documents of which are nude female figures in which the belly is often swollen. At times these figures also bear a deep groove in the protuberance that must be a representation of the vulva. The particular care given to the annotation of the sexual organs fosters the belief that most of the female statuettes expressed fecundity or fertility. A small infantile bone found incorporated in a statuette has been interpreted as the magic rite of a women seeking

the birth of a son. The discovery of a certain number of figurines in a hut destroyed by fire has led to the theory that this was a sanctuary dedicated to the protective spirits of maternity, or perhaps a parturition hut. Ancient Japanese literature often mentions the huts where women about to give birth were isolated from the community, as were women in menstruation, newlyweds, and even the wounded and moribund, because of a taboo connected with the effusion of blood. Other scholars see in the statuettes the iconography of a primitive deity of the Ainu tradition, or of the ancient Japanese household gods; but it is extremely doubtful that the Ainu or the Japanese, in such a remote period, has developed an iconographic conception of the divine that later disappeared completely. As far as is known, religious iconography in the archipelago was a late development, coming only with the importation of Buddhism.

On the whole, the theory that the statuettes were used for fertility rites is probably the most valid. The discovery of stone phallic symbols seems to confirm this idea. Moreover, these are ideas that have persisted in Japan up to fairly recent times; even in the last century, orgiastic fertility rites were celebrated in the Japanese countryside. Fertility beliefs are also connected with the powers of certain divinities of the native Shinto cult. The statuettes probably sum up the gradual development of Japanese religiosity, from the primitive cults concerning human and animal fecundity — characteristic of the hunting and food-gathering populations — to those that, after the adoption of agriculture in Japan, included the fertility of the crops.

Bronze and Iron Ages

The agricultural revolution came rather late to Japan, where it can be dated only from the middle of the first millennium B.C. It is from this age on that the Jomon communities seem to have reached their widest extension, simultaneously settling down into a village life, and no longer subject to periodic moves. In the process of social settlement, the economy of the Jomon groups passed from one of consumption to one of production, from indiviual or domestic activity to really cooperative organization. In the southern regions, however, this transformation was no sooner achieved than Jomon died out, replaced by a new culture of distinctly different type. The new culture is called Yayoi, from the first findings in the Yayoi district of Tokyo in the last century; with its coming, the culture of the ancient countryside, with its shell mounds, disappeared completely. Once primary activities such as hunting and fishing fell firmly into the background. The new settlements were agricultural villages founded on cultivable plains or on land near sources of water. A hoe and plough agriculture, based on intensive cultivation and irrigation, was initiated, with rice as the main crop. The dwellings of the new culture had their floors either on the ground or raised above it. The first huts, either circular or oblong, were at ground level and consisted of a series of crossed poles on which the beams of a pavilion-type roof were set. The second type, with the floor set above ground level on poles driven into the earth, must have been somewhat similar to a boarded pile fence, with exterior stairs. The constructions at first had only one room; later the interior was divided into several rooms by means of partitions joined to the poles of the frame and to the central pillar. The sloping roofs were made of vegetable fiber, straw, and wood. These huts were the ancient precursors of the light and airy Japanese house of the historic period.

Industrial equipment consisted of stone tools in well-smoothed shapes at first, among which were specific agricultural tools such as the quadrangular ax and crescent-shaped knives. Later on, with the increasing spread of metal, bronze objects and tools were used. Pottery was made

on the wheel and took many different shapes; there are specimens with tall pedestals and others shaped like double jars, used for the boiling of rice. Painted decoration replaced the classical relief ornamentation of Jomon pottery. Stone and terra-cotta urns were used as containers for the dead, in necropolises that were set far away from the villages. The entire cultural context is so fundamentally different from the Jomon that any idea of relatively rapid progress, effected by the Neolithic populations by means of some hypothetical contact with the continent, must be discounted. The qualitative change points rather to a superimposition, to the entrance of new groups into the archipelago.

Anthropology has verified the presence of Mongol elements in the new culture, but has not yet been able to ascertain the origin, number, and character of the migratory waves. An examination of the archaeological findings suggests that the new civilization was not formed through a single wave of migrants, but through infiltrations that lasted for centuries. In the long range of time from the third century B.C. to the third century A.D., Japan was exposed to a flow of ethnic and cultural elements that spread from the northern coasts of Kyushu through the central and southern regions of the archipelago. North of the Kanto plain — that is, beyond a border line about 155 miles north of Tokyo — the Jomon culture survived, lasting in certain regions up to the end of the first millennium of the Christian era.

The origins of the Yayoi civilization are thought to be somewhere in the insular territories of southeast Asia or in the coastal centers of the Far East. At one time it was thought that the spread of the culture could be attributed to migrant populations from Indochina or Indonesia. Besides the anthropological affinities that the Japanese have with the populations of Australasia, there is also the proof furnished by the cultivation of rice, the light wooden architecture of indisputably southern origin, and the characteristic quadrangular, smooth-stone ax. It has since been found, however, that both the cultivation of rice and the quadrangular ax were already characteristic of central-eastern China in the late Neolithic Age, as were other techniques and objects to be found in Yayoi Japan, such as the potter's wheel, the system of double jars for the cooking of rice, the vases with pedestals, and the crescent-shaped knives. The Chinese influence emerges as predominant in the Yayoi cultural complex, and mirrors and coins of Chinese origin, dating from the Han dynasty (206 B.C.–A.D. 9), have been found in Yayoi sites.

The most valid hypothesis today is thus that of a cultural radiation from China. The southern component, indisputable in the Yayoi civilization and well documented by the architecture, among other things, suggests that the radiation took place from southern China, in an age when the formation of the first Chinese empire (third century B.C.) had begun to exert strong pressure on the preexisting southern communities, many of which may have fled by sea to Korea and Japan. The results of ethnological and linguistic research, which has traced many elements of this age in Japan to obvious parentage in southern China, indicate this also. Other influences seem to have come directly from Korea, where agricultural civilization had in the meantime mixed with elements of southern origin. A Korean influence is demonstrated by the introduction at this time of megalithic construction practices, the use of large stone slabs and masses that seems to derive from the funerary customs of nomadic populations on the periphery of the northeastern steppes.

Yayoi civilization was a mosaic, then, formed from a variety of ethnic and cultural components. Absolute fusion was not realized even in the archipelago itself; a sharp cultural and political division can be noted between eastern and western Japan. Archaeologically speaking, there were two great and distinct cultural centers: in the southwest, bronze ceremonial weapons, such as swords, spear points, and halberd points, dominate; in the east, the ceremonial tools consist of symbolic bronze bells. Up to the present time, these findings have led to no definite conclusions about the centers. That of the southwest,

in Kyushu, may have derived from different cultural sources than that of the east, in Yamato, and may have had a more or less independent process of development. Nor can a clear political importance be ascribed to the two large territorial groupings. They may represent the first tribal unions in the country. Almost certainly in this epoch the agricultural communities were organized in socially larger groups, and the specialization of jobs and techniques — in the making of agricultural tools, for example — had led to the formation of separate categories of artisans, from which the first artistic and professional corporations, the Be, sprang up; these are spoken of in the later indigenous historiographical tradition.

The working of metal was the most obvious new element in the Yayoi epoch. Metal production had not yet developed on a large scale, however, and was limited to articles of an ornamental character and to symbolic instruments for religious ceremonies. Because of the subtlety and fragility of their blades, it is certain that the arms from this period were not put to practical use. The fact that they were buried in large numbers suggests that they were meant to be used to protect the soil from raids and calamities or to propitiate spirits for the prosperity of the people. Fertility beliefs connected with the spear points have been handed down by tradition; in fact, Japanese mythology attributes the formation of the first island in the Japanese archipelago to the point of a lance. Some corresponding magical or ritual value must also have been attached to the bronze bells, the *dotaku*. As may be seen from the example in Figure 4, these were objects of an elongated cone form, with an opening at the top by which they might be hung. The presence of a clapper in some specimens seems to indicate that the *dotaku* were originally real bells. Their prototypes are found in China and Korea, although the forms differ quite a bit.

In Japan they passed through a singular evolution, taking on much larger dimensions. The most ancient examples are from four to eight inches high, but later examples reach a height of over three feet. As they grew larger, the objects seem to have lost their function as well. No trace of the clapper can be found, and even the sonority and the percussive element are compromised by the presence of holes on the sides formed through fusion. At this point the *dotaku* probably began to play the role of symbolic instruments in magical-religious ceremonies, as their discovery in deep ditches suggests. They may have been ritually buried, with the object of propitiating the forces of nature. As a fertility symbol they probably represented the female element, and along these lines scholars have connected them with the ancient Indochinese *kosa*, which were used as a kind of hat or covering for phallic symbols, the *linga*. The outer sides of the *dotaku* have simple decoration, finely engraved or in relief, made up of linear and outline motifs, in parallel bands and squares, inside which there is often a schematic and stylized decoration of a naturalistic bent, with human and animal figures depicting scenes of daily life: hunting, fishing, farming, or domestic activities. There are recurrent figures of hunters — bearing bows, shooting arrows, and running, preceded by packs of hounds; there are groups of men in boats, and long processions of fish, fowl, and ruminant beasts. Scenes of daily life or representations of human and animal figures also occur at times in the pottery of the Yayoi epoch. A series of terra-cotta jars of uncertain intended use bear masks and human faces obtained by a rudimentary relief technique, as well as engraved or colored forms in outline.

Megalithic Monuments

The funerary rite of burial in jars, already noted in the Jomon epoch, spread more widely in the Yayoi period as a consequence of megalithic funerary customs, which introduced simple tomb structures, made of

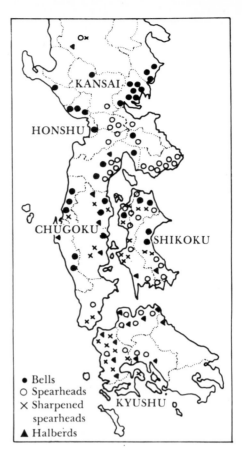

Map of the archaeological sites of the Yayoi Period. The signs refer to the geographical distribution of various bronze objects (bells, spearheads, and halberds).

Map of the distribution of megalithic tombs of the Kofun Period (fourth to sixth centuries A.D.)

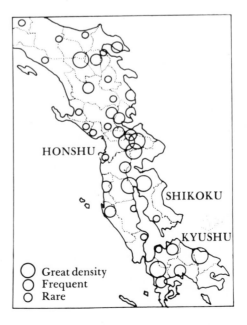

Now all the Sky-Kami deigned to bid He-Who-Invites and She-Who-Invites [Izanagi and Izaname] to make and consolidate the drifting earth, saying, "There is the Fruitful-Reed-Plain-Land-of-Fresh-Rice-Ears-of-Thousand-Autumns. Go and set it in order." So, a Sky-Jewel-Spear whose staff was of coral having been granted them, the pair took stand upon the Floating-Sky-Bridge (or, as some say, in the midst of the Sky-Mist).

On the Bridge the two Kami held counsel, after which, saying, "Lo, there is something here like floating oil; perhaps there is an island in its midst," they dipped down the Sky-Jewel-Spear and moved it about till they found the sea plain, and searching for a land, they stirred the briny silt till it was all *kowaro-kowaro*, saying, "Surely there must be a land!" When they drew the spear up, the drippings from its point piled up and formed the Island Self-Curdling [Onagoro]. At that they rejoiced and drew up the spear, saying, "Good! There is a land!"

They descended and dwelt in this island and erected a palace eight *hiro* long, and they set up a Sky-Pillar and made the Island Self-Curdling the Pillar of the Land's center. Now they desired to become husband and wife and to produce countries, and would have cohabited, but knew not how. However there came to them a wagtail which beat together its head and its tail, and the two, imitating it, obtained knowledge of the manner of sexual intercourse. He-Who-Invites then asked his younger sister She-Who-Invites, "In what fashion is your body formed?" She replied, "In the growing of my body there is one part which grew not joined together, which is the female source-spot." Then said He-Who-Invites, "In the growing of my body there is one part which grew superfluous, which is the male source-spot. Would it not be well, therefore, that I insert that part of my body which grew superfluous, the male source-spot, into the part of your body which grew not joined together, the female source-spot, and procreate territories?" She-Who-Invites replied, "It would be well." Then said He-Who-Invites, "To this end let us go around about this Sky-Pillar and mutually meeting, join together our august parts in cohabitation." Having thus agreed, He-Who-Invites said, "Do you go around to the right; I will go to the left." So, the male Kami going to the left and the female Kami to the right, when they had gone around separately and met on the same side, She-Who-Invites speaking first, said, "O comely and lovable youth!" At that He-Who-Invites said, "O comely and lovable maiden!" When they had thus spoken, he was displeased and said, "I am the man and of right should have been the first to speak. How is it that you, on the contrary, spoke first? This was unlucky. We should go around again." Nevertheless, the female Kami took the hand of the male Kami and they became united as husband and wife and began to cohabit, and begot a son named Leech [Hiruko]. This child did not please them, since even at the age of three years it could not stand upright; so they took a boat made of reeds, and laying the child in it, set it adrift, abandoning it to the winds and the currents. Next they procreated Foam-Island [Aha-shima], which is not reckoned among their offspring.

They then took counsel together, saying, "These children to whom we gave birth are not good," and reascending to the Sky-Kami, they announced this fact in the august place. Thereon the Sky-*Ancestor*-Kami, having made grand divination, decreed, "How can one think of the woman speaking first!" and bade them descend and make the trial again. So, descending, they again went around the pillar as before when He-Who-Invites spoke first, saying, "Ah, what a fair and lovely maiden!" Then She-Who-Invites said, "Ah, what a fair and lovely youth!" When they had thus spoken they cohabited and gave birth to the island of my shame [Ahaji].

Wheeler: *Sacred Scriptures* (*pp. 5–7*)

blocks and slabs of stone and set on the ground. They have been related to analogous forms in southern Korea. It is thought they are indications of a new cultural wave that, with the megalithic builders, reached the most remote regions of the Japanese archipelago. The blocks of stone used are colossal. Both tombs (*dolmen*) and tall monoliths (*menhir*), perhaps used by solar cults, were raised. The megalithic age lasted a long time in Japan, and developed in a vast geographic area from Kyushu through the interior of Honshu. The *dolmen* in Figure 5 is found in the prefecture of Nara, and was probably built in the seventh century A.D. The masses of stone and the huge boulders used as a covering form an inner room in which the sarcophagi, in the form of jars, were deposited.

Megalithic techniques were not limited to funerary functions, however. The *menhir* frequently set into the earth poetically evoke the ancient myth of the divine progenitorial couple of Japan, Izanagi and Izaname, who reputedly descended from the heavens onto the island formed by the point of a lance to erect an "august celestial pillar." Having thus established the axis of the world, they performed around it the magic rite of fecundity. Izanagi and Izaname are the divinities given credit for the creation of the Japanese archipelago, the sea, hell, and the vault of heaven, as well as the principal gods who populated the earth. These latter include the goddess of the sun, the guardian of Japan, the "central land of the plains of reeds and the luxuriant shoots of rice," as well as the ancestor of the Japanese emperor. The stone circles and the stones set into the earth imply ancient sun cults connected with the traditional solar conceptions of Japanese religion as transmitted by mythology and tradition.

Another religious key can be used to interpret the great stone monument illustrated in Figure 6, the Masuda no Iwafune (stone boat), which dates from the sixth or seventh century A.D. The theme of boats, which frequently recurs in tomb decorations, is related to the rites and beliefs concerning the voyage of the dead to the other world, according to the typical horizontal cosmology of sea populations, in which the afterlife is set not under the earth, but across the seas. Shinto, Japan's indigenous cult, has perpetuated the purification liturgy, in which the boats, loaded with sins, periodically move toward the sea. The Masuda no Iwafune may have been used symbolically for a ritual of this kind. It is monumental, over twenty-six feet high. The colossal size of the mass eloquently reveals the availability of groups of people for collective work in an early epoch. It is hardly the effort of a pacific agricultural society organized on a cooperative basis; the realization of such monuments implies a rather strongly authoritarian organization, with a ruling class, whose basically agricultural population might be utilized periodically in heavy-duty service. The Masuda no Iwafune is a symbol of Japan's passage from the Bronze Age to the Iron Age. Even more indicative of the new social organization are the monumental tumulus tombs of the period roughly from the fourth to the seventh century A.D. The tumulus of the "emperor" Nintoku (Figure 7) is 525 yards long, 333 yards wide and 114 feet high, and the tumuli of the "emperors" Ojin and Richu, in the prefecture of Osaka, are almost as large. There are ten thousand other tumuli scattered from Kyushu through Honshu north to the region of Kanto, and while they are not as colossal as the three just mentioned, they are thoroughly imposing, nonetheless.

Tumulus Tombs

Because of its characteristic structures, the epoch following the Yayoi is called Kofun, (ancient tombs). During this period new funerary practices spread over the archipelago. The *dolmen* tradition of the

6. Masuda no Iwafune, a megalithic monument in the form of a boat. Height 26 feet 3 inches. Sixth or seventh century A.D. Prefecture of Nara.

Following pages:
7. Aerial view of the tomb of the "emperor" Nintoku. The tumulus, in a keyhole form, is surrounded by a moat. Length 525 yards, width 333 yards, height 114 feet. Fifth century A.D. Sakai, Prefecture of Osaka.

6

Bronze Age was continued, but their simple structures are flanked, in this later megalithic phase, by chamber tombs and sepulchers cut out of the rock, stone sarcophagi, and, above all, by chamber and corridor tombs covered by high piles of earth. The new tomb structures derived from a funerary tradition found throughout the entire continental Far East, as far as Manchuria and Mongolia, a tradition that entered the archipelago through Korean, and probably Chinese, influence. Many of the practices used were common in China, and the instruments and objects of funerary equipment are clearly of Chinese derivation. Among these the iron weapons stand out; they are the precursors of the spears and sabers of the historic period.

8. Interior of the funerary chamber of a Daibo tumulus tomb, with a wall painted in geometric motifs. Sixth century A.D. Prefecture of Kumamoto.

8

Schematic drawing and plan of the chamber and corridor tomb of the Otsuka tumulus. Fourth to sixth centuries A.D. (Kofun Period:) Prefecture of Okayama.

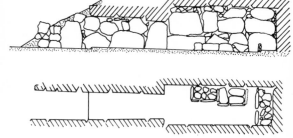

9. Wall painting inside the Takehara tumulus tomb. The scene, framed by two insignias of rank, shows a small boat on the waves of the sea. Above it are the figures of two horses, and that of a groom or a warrior. Sixth century A.D. (Kofun Period). Island of Kyushu.

The tumulus tombs are generally circular or oblong, but their most distinctive shape is that of a gigantic keyhole, with the front part of trapezoidal form and the part behind it approximately circular. As the aerial view in Figure 7 illustrates, the tumulus is surrounded by a sort of moat filled with water, to protect the tomb from violation. Construction within the tumulus generally consists of a sepulchral chamber of elongated form, which is at times preceded by an atrium or an access corridor. These are built of masses and slabs of stone laid one atop another, or of simple dry-stone walls. Figure 8 shows a slab niche inside the tumulus tomb at Daibo, its back wall painted with triangles alternately filled in with red. The engraved or painted decora-

9

10. Detail of the face of a funerary statue, one of the *saruseki* (stone monkeys). Height 3 feet 3 inches. Sixth or seventh century A.D. Prefecture of Nara.

THE HANIWA

28th year, Winter, 10th month, 5th day. Yamato-hiko no Mikoto, the Emperor's younger brother by the mother's side, died.

11th month, 2nd day. Yamato-hiko was buried at Tsukizaka in Musa. Thereupon his personal attendants were assembled, and were all buried alive upright in the precinct of the misasagi. For several days they died not, but wept and wailed day and night. At last they died and rotted. Dogs and crows gathered and ate them.

The Emperor, hearing the sound of their weeping and wailing, was grieved in heart, and commanded his high officers, saying: — "It is a very painful thing to force those whom one has loved in life to follow him in death. Though it be an ancient custom, why follow it, if it is bad? From this time forward, take counsel so as to put a stop to the following of the dead."

30th year, Spring, 1st month, 6th day. The Emperor commanded Inishiki no Mikoto and Oho-tarashi-hiko no Mikoto, saying: — "Do ye each tell me the thing ye would dearly like to have." The elder Prince said: — "I should like to have a bow and arrows." The younger Prince said: — "I should like to have the Imperial Dignity." Thereupon the Emperor commanded, saying: — "Let the desire of each of you be complied with." So a bow and arrows were given to Inishiki no Mikoto, and a decree was addressed to Oho-tarashi hiko no Mikoto, saying: — "Thou must succeed to Our Dignity."

32nd year, Autumn, 7th month, 6th day. The Empress Hibasu-hime no Mikoto died.

One version has Hibasu ne no Mikoto. Some time before the burial, the Emperor commanded his Ministers, saying: — "We have already recognized that the practice of following the dead is not good. What should now be done in performing this burial?" Thereupon Nomi no Sukune came forward and said: — "It is not good to bury living men upright at the tumulus of a prince. How can such a practice be handed down to posterity? I beg leave to propose an expedient which I will submit to Your Majesty." So he sent messengers to summon up from the Land of Idzumo a hundred men of the clay-workers' Be. He himself directed the men of the clay-workers' Be to take clay and form therewith shapes of men, horses, and various objects, which he presented to the Emperor, saying: — "Henceforward let it be the law for future ages to substitute things of clay for living men, and to set them up at tumuli." Then the Emperor was greatly rejoiced, and commanded Nomi no Sukune, saying: — "Thy expedient hath greatly pleased Our heart." So the things of clay were first set up at the tomb of Hibasu-hime no Mikoto. And a name was given to these clay objects. They were called *Haniwa*.

Another name is *Tatemono*.

Aston: *Nihongi* (*pp.* 178–181)

tion with geometric or highly stylized naturalistic motifs frequently appears on the interior walls of the tombs. Among the geometric themes are triangles, circles, radial and curvilinear motifs, which suggest a magical-symbolic interpretation, often of a solar character. Alternating with the geometric ornament, and sometimes predominating, is decoration with a realistic touch: human figures, horses, shields, quivers, and boats (at times depicted with people on board). An example of this type is the painting in the tomb of Takehara (Figure 9).

Another sort of sepulchral decoration adorns the entranceway or the interior of some tombs, most often those built with masses of rough stone. These are elementary compositions; those at the entranceways are executed with a rudimentary technique of flat, low relief, and depict simplified human figures, sometimes armed with bow and quiver, in outline form and in rigid frontal positions. Inside the tombs there are stone sculptures in the round, carved from cylindrical blocks; these represent human figures with large heads. The face, with its essential features, is barely traced, and the rest of the body is rendered in a rough and heavy manner. The example in Figure 10 belongs to a small group of male and female statues that, because of their only roughly human appearance, have been called *saruseki* (stone monkeys). Such sculptures, used specifically for tombs, seem to belong to a genre of art that spread in the wake of megalithic funerary art, if not in imitation of the well-known Chinese custom of decorating the entrances and access ways of tombs with statues. But the coarseness of their execution and their rather slight diffusion in the archipelago may perhaps be explained by the absence of any earlier local tradition of sculpture.

Haniwa and Funerary Objects and Furnishings

However, when we examine the funerary cults in the Japanese archipelago, we do find works of artistic value. We refer particularly to the *haniwa* which were deposited on the tumuli, set in circles from the top down along the slopes to the base. As the Japanese term implies, *haniwa* were at first simply terra-cotta cylinders. About sixteen inches high, they were placed in the tumulus and around it, either to prevent landslides or to build a protective barrier against the spirits of evil, or as a sign of the symbolic limits of the tomb. Later cylinders, however, have another element on top of them, a terra-cotta element, molded in the shape of a human figure. Although these can be classified as funerary objects, they were not strictly speaking a part of the tomb, and have never been found inside the tomb chambers, at least not until a more modern period. From a remote time the Japanese maintained that the *haniwa* were the images of sacrificial victims who had once been killed to honor the dead, in correspondence with an ancient Chinese funerary custom. Human sacrifice is frequently to be noted in China in tombs of the Shang (sixteenth and fifteenth centuries B.C.) and Chou (eleventh to the third century B.C.) dynasties, and at its abolition it was supplanted by the custom of setting wooden or clay statuettes next to the dead.

When the meaning of the *haniwa* had already been lost in Japan, it was thought that they represented a substitute form analogous to the Chinese one, especially since Chinese sources themselves stated that in Japan human sacrifice was practiced up until the first centuries of the Christian era. Chinese historians attributed the custom to the Japanese not on the basis of verified facts, however, but as a generic indication of "Japanese barbarity." Yet archaeology has not yet found any indication that funerary sacrifice was practiced in the archipelago. No evidence has been found of bones from human or animal victims who may have accompanied the dead, inside or outside the tombs. In China, the funerary statuettes were always deposited

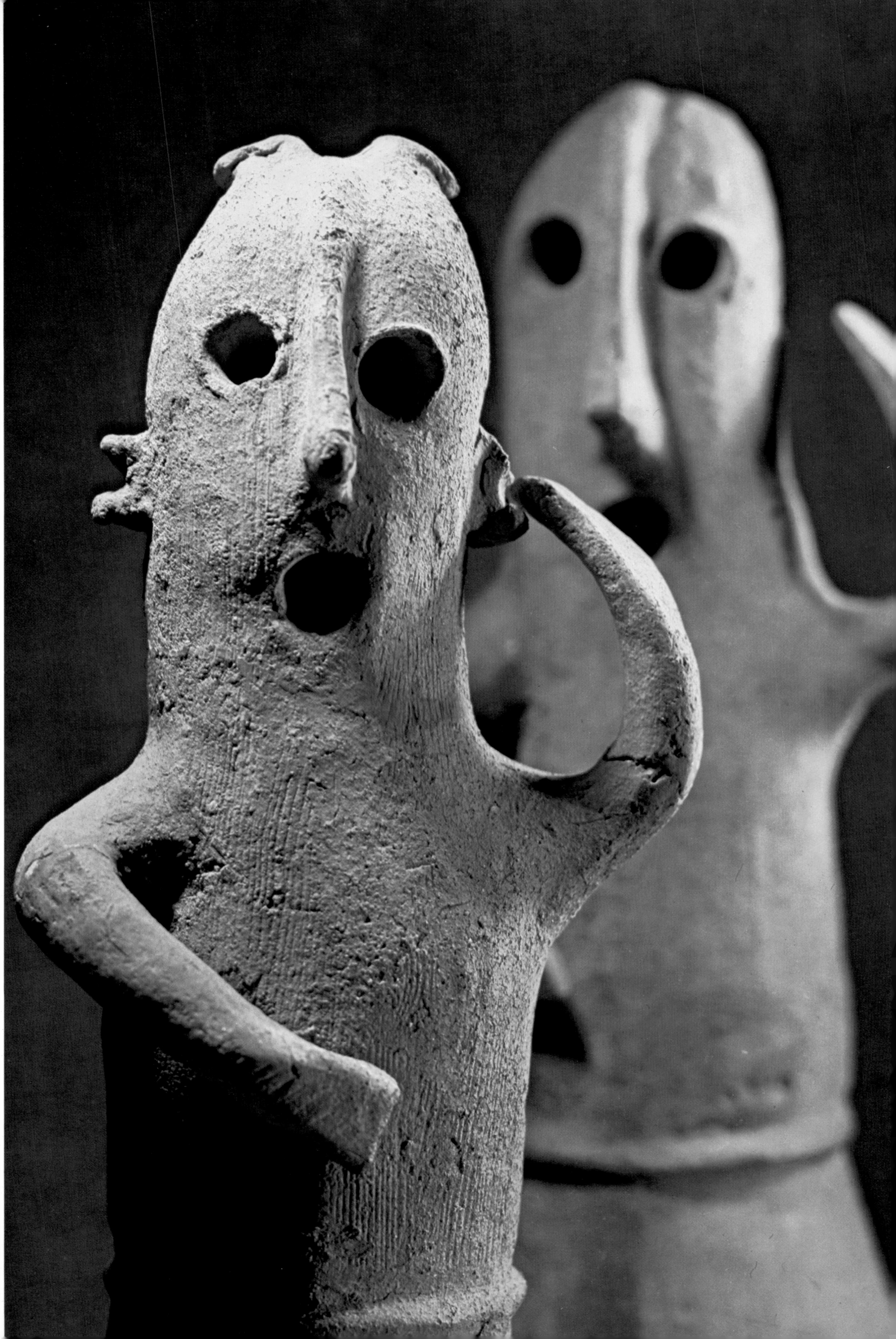

11. Clay funerary statues called *haniwa* (terra-cotta cylinders). They were placed on the tumulus tombs as dedicatory objects. Height of the figure on the right, 25.31 inches; the figure on the left 22.56 inches. Fifth or sixth century A.D. From the Prefecture of Gunma. (Tokyo National Museum).

12. Clay *haniwa* statuette of a female personage. Fifth or sixth century A.D. (Kofun Period). From the Prefecture of Gunma (Tokyo National Museum).

13. Clay *haniwa* statuette of a warrior. Height 25.27 inches. Sixth century A.D. From Kami-chujo, Kumagaya, Prefecture of Saitama. (Tokyo National Museum).

inside the tomb. Since the *haniwa* were set outside, the Japanese of the historic period explained that sacrificial victims had been buried in a standing position in the earth of the tumuli, and that nothing remained of them because they had been devoured by animals. The standing position sacrifice was practiced in Japan, in fact, but as a rite of propitiation, rather than for funerary purposes. Up to fairly recent times the custom of the *hito-bashira* (human columns), buried in a standing position inside the wall structures of bridges or dangerous banks, was traditional. A number of elements seem to have contributed to the belief that *haniwa* were substitutes for bloody sacrifices.

While it is true that at certain moments Chinese influences imposed themselves directly (in Japan the custom of placing one or more clay or cloth puppets in coffins to keep the dead company has survived up to the modern age: it undoubtedly springs from Chinese practice) a more likely source of the *haniwa* were the *kam-menye-baba*, the statues that the nomadic populations of the continent erected on the tombs of their dead. During the protohistorical period, they were a well-documented custom of the central-Asian territories from which many Japanese customs of the Kofun era originate. Although the *kam-menye-baba* may have been the origin of *haniwa* in human form, the repertory of forms was enlarged in Japan, perhaps because of Chinese influence, to include animal figures and the reproduction of objects.

The manufacture of the *haniwa* gave rise to several production centers in various regions of the archipelago, and developed for a period of about three or four centuries. The most ancient specimen of a cylinder is probably of the third century A.D., while those in the form of human and animal figures, the reproductions of buildings, boats, and other objects of common or ceremonial use, date from the fifth and sixth centuries. The *haniwa* human figures first retained much of the ancient cylinder-form structure. Figure 11 shows two examples made from such tubes; they have the appearance of astonished ghosts or grotesque hooded figures. It may be that they are images of dancers; the use of long, curving arms to indicate a dancer is a figurative stereotype of east Asia.

The later *haniwa* reveal greater articulation in their modeling, and have a more realistic look. In the obvious attempt to give the figures rhythm and to avoid otherwise static and rigid positions, some examples have the arms held out or up, in the act of holding an object or making a gesture. The face, usually colored red and sometimes tattooed, is treated only in its essential features; two round or almond-shaped holes indicate the eyes and a perforation traces the mouth. The eyebrows and nose are often rendered with particular care; the latter is for the most part straight and prominent, almost as if to indicate the physical sign of a noble race. The ears are usually in relief, but in the cruder examples they are rendered by simple holes. The *haniwa* were executed in series, and therefore have little individual characterization, yet the images are not without expression. This is sometimes austere and remote, if the oblong cuts of the mouth and the eyes are rectilinear. If the cuts of the eyes are round and the mouth is open in the shape of a half-moon, the expression is comic and grotesque. The expressive means are simple, for the most part limited by the technique of cutting, and the characterization is hardly ever obtained by manipulation of the plastic elements, so the expression, although it sometimes succeeds in being incisive, is always pervaded by a sense of innocence or ingenuousness. The human figure is often depicted only to the bust, especially the female images, but there are frequent examples of entire figures, seated or standing, which represent both men and women. There is no lack of nude figures, which almost always treat the sexual organs with anatomical explicitness. More often, however, the figures are completely clothed. The men's dress consists of close-fitting jackets and wide trousers tied to the knee, and the women's of bodices and bell-shaped skirts. The example in Figure 12 probably followed closely the fashion of the time, from the headgear to the trimmings of the clothes. These fashions have affinities with those in China in the epoch between the Han and Sui dynasties (A.D. 220–589). Close attention is given to the treatment of the ornaments, the tattoos, and above all the helmets, armor, and weapons of the numerous warrior figures. These are reproduced with graphic precision in every detail (Figure 13). This is the world of the military aristocracy, which in the Kofun epoch established its supremacy over the agricultural populations of the archipelago and handed down the monuments of their dominion to posterity throught the funerary tumuli.

Inside the sepulchral chambers, and often also in the sarcophagi of the tumulus tombs, quite rich funerary objects and furnishings have been found. These include terra-cotta and porcelain vases; bronze, iron, silver, and gold instruments and jewels; and other ornamental objects of hard stone and glass. Lacquered furnishings, drapes, and fabrics have been found as well, together with a great amount of weapons and armor.

From an artistic point of view, however, the most important objects are the bronze mirrors, the crowning achievement of the metal technique of the time. Believed to have magical-symbolic value, they were appropriated as emblems by the solar cult and the imperial ranks. In Japanese mythology, the mirror, together with the sword

THE ORIGIN OF THE MIRROR AS THE EMBLEM OF THE SUN GODDESS

So thereupon the Heaven-Shining-Great-August-Deity [the sun goddess Amaterasu]. . . closed behind her the door of the Heavenly-Rock-Dwelling, made it fast, and retired, then the whole Plain of High Heaven was obscured and all the Central Land of Reed-Plains darkened. Owing to this, eternal night prevailed . . . .

Therefore did the eight hundred myriad Deities assemble in a divine assembly in the bed of the Tranquil River of Heaven, and bid the Deity Thought-Includer, child of the High-August-Producing-Wondrous-Deity think of a plan, assembling the long-singing birds of eternal night and making them sing, taking the hard rocks of Heaven from the riverbed of the Tranquil River of Heaven, and taking the iron from the Heavenly Metal-Mountains, calling in the smith Ama-tsu-ma-ra, charging Her Augustness I-shi-ko-ri-do-me to make a mirror. . . . Her Augustness Heavenly-Alarming-Female hanging round her the heavenly clubmoss from the Heavenly Mount Kagu as a sash, and making the heavenly spindle-tree her headdress, and binding the leaves of the bamboo-grass of the Heavenly Mount Kagu in a posy for her hands, laying a sounding-board before the door of the Heavenly Rock-Dwelling, and stamping till she made it resound and doing as if possessed by a Deity, and pulling out the nipples of her breasts, pushing down her skirt-string to her private parts. Then the Plain of High Heaven shook, and the eight hundred myriad Deities laughed together. Hereupon the Heaven-Shining-Great-August-Deity was amazed, and, slightly opening the door of the Heavenly Rock-Dwelling, spoke thus from the inside: "Methought that owing to my retirement the Plain of Heaven would be dark, and likewise the Central Land of Reed-Plains would all be dark: how then is it that the Heavenly-Alarming-Female makes merry, and that likewise the eight hundred myriad Deities laugh?"

Then the Heavenly-Alarming-Female spoke, saying: "We rejoice and are glad because there is a Deity more illustrious than thine Augustness." While she was thus speaking, two other Deities pushed forward the mirror and respectfully showed it to the Heaven-shining-Great-August-Deity, whereupon the Heavenly-Shining-Great-August-Deity, more and more astonished, gradually came forth from the door and gazed upon it, whereupon the Heavenly-Hand-Strength-Male-Deity, who was standing hidden, took her august hand and drew her out. . . . So when the Heaven-Shining-Great-August-Deity had come forth, both the Plain of High Heaven and the Central-Land-of-Reed-Plains of course again became light.

Chamberlain: *Ko-ji-ki* (II edition, *pp.* 64–70)

14. Bronze mirror with geometric decoration. Seventh century A.D. From Okinoshima, Prefecture of Fukuoka.

Following pages:
15. View of the Shinto sanctuary at Ise, known as Kotai Jingu. Dedicated to the sun goddess Amaterasu, the sanctuary has traditionally been linked with the imperial cult. Ise, Prefecture of Mie.

Pages 40–41:
16. The roofs and ridge decorations of the Izumo Shinto sanctuary, known as Izumo Taisha. Taisha-machi, Prefecture of Shimane.

and the jewel, were delivered by the goddess of the sun to her grandson Ninigi, as symbols of her divine sovereignty, when he received the mandate to descend from the sky onto the islands of Japan to establish the supremacy of the sun and set down the bases of the Japanese empire. The mirrors (Figure 14) are shaped like disks, with one smooth, reflecting surface. Lacking a handle, they have a central appendage on the back, much like a knob with a hole cut in it, through which a cord may be put, to hang or hold the mirror. On the back also there is normally a decoration in various relief motifs. The most ancient specimens seem to be identical in form and decoration with the Chinese mirrors of the Han dynasty. Some perhaps came directly from China, as the first local production was vastly inferior in workmanship and in quality of design. Many examples must have been imported from Manchuria or Korea.

The indigenous production improved considerably in quality later

on, but the decoration continued to imitate that of the Chinese models. At times the imitation is well done, however, as in the case of certain mirrors that carefully and faithfully reproduce the simple geometric compositions of the Han dynasty originals. This is the case with the mirror in the illustration, which combines the symmetrically arranged "L" and "T" motifs with spiral and curvilinear motifs. Also worth mention is the repetition of iconographic and symbolic motifs, particularly Taoist ones, which frequently recur in the Chinese mirrors of the Six Dynasties period (A.D. 420–589). The Japanese artisans seem not really to understand the intimate meaning of these motifs; they reproduce them in a servile and sometimes clumsy way, attracted only by the formal beauty of the design.

Once the stage of pure imitation is past, however, the mirrors are distinguished from the Chinese models by their greater formal and stylistic elaboration; and while the fashions differentiate themselves because of size and the addition of particular elements, motifs and themes of typically local taste are introduced into the decoration. The same realistic, almost narrative, style can be noted in the bronze *dotaku* and on other pottery; hunting and dancing scenes, figures of warriors, representations of houses are important. Depictions of buildings on the mirrors, together with the *haniwa* of buildings, are major sources of information on the architecture of the time.

Early Architecture

There is comprehensive documentation to verify that during this age considerable progress in construction techniques was made, although stone and masonry building remained limited almost exclusively to funerary purposes. The religious architecture of Shinto, the Japanese indigenous cult, adheres to the building types of the time, and the sanctuaries at Ise and Izumo (Figures 15–17), though they have undergone periodic reconstruction, keep the architectural conceptions of protohistoric Japan intact. The perishable construction materials, the techniques of joining and assembling wood, the structure of the pillars, wooden partitions, beams and double-sloped roofs of vegetable fiber, clearly relate the basic types of religious architecture to the common structures of ancient domestic architecture.

"August house" or "house substitute" are the names ancient Shinto used to designate its sanctuaries, which were dedicated to both celestial or terrestrial divinities, and to spirits and symbols of the natural and human world. From the great sanctuaries of the ancient national cult to the humblest of the rural districts, the thousands of buildings of worship scattered over the Japanese countryside can be identified essentially by the type of shrine used to house the "body" of the god, in whatever visible form it manifested itself: a mirror, a sword, a stone, or a simple writing tablet. Shinto practice was somewhat similar to the Chinese custom of ancestor worship. The connection between sanctuary and dwelling place, and even with the ancient imperial residences, has never been broken. In the entire history of Shinto the sacred place has never been conceived as a monument erected in honor of the divine, but rather as a simple receptacle of the god, revealed on earth through a symbol or an object. This explains the rather small dimensions of the religious buildings, which mirror even in their scale the modest ancient houses of a basically rural population. In the historical period the hut with its floor raised on pillars is the prototype of the Shinto sanctuary; the religious building merely has slightly larger dimensions and clearer plans, and its raised floors are better stabilized.

The oldest type of Shinto architectural structure, represented by the Izumo sanctuary, still has a characteristic central pillar, the cosmic interpretation of which — that is, as the axis of the world — can

hardly be separated from its functional reference to the ancient architecture of the huts. The floor of the building consists of a platform, at first square and later rectangular, held up by pillars set into the earth. On these pillars, which rise to the height of the building, rests the double-sloped roof, covered with rice straw or tree bark. The pillars serve as a reinforcement for the frame and are, together with the architraves, the only support for the edifice. The wall as a rule has no supporting function, but serves only as a curtain. Monumentality in the vertical sense is therefore precluded; any monumental effects should be sought rather in the articulation of many edifices together and in the combined structures of their roofs. The Ise sanctuary, dedicated to the sun goddess Amaterasu, the ancestral divinity of the imperial family, is an attempt to reproduce the primitive type of imperial residence, the so-called palace hall, where the divinity had at first been the object of worship before a distinct sacred room was dedicated to her. The circumstances surrounding the building of this sanctuary are painted in a famous legend. The "emperor" Suijin (A.D. 230–258), fearing that the reason for a terrible pestilence that was raging over the land was to be found in the sun goddess' resentment at being worshiped in a hall in the imperial palace together with another divinity, Yamato no Okumi dana, separated the cults and placed the worship hall of Amaterasu at a certain distance from the court. Under the reign of his successor Suinin (A.D. 259–290) the sanctuary was definitively established at Ise.

The shrine was first built during the third and fourth centuries, but its definitive structural lines, which can be seen more or less in the structures as they stand today, were fixed in the seventh century. The buildings of the shrine itself are distributed symmetrically within their enclosures. The constructions rest on rectangular wooden platforms held up by pillars set into the earth. The jutting roof, with its straight slopes, rests on these same pillars, and the gable is finished at each end by bargeboards along the slopes, which are extended into a scissors-like crosswork at the top. The structures used for worship consist of two similar compounds, the inner shrine, or *naigu*, and the outer shrine, or *gegu*. Each is reached by passing through a portal at its outer limit, a schematic post and lintel structure somewhat in the form of a Greek "p" (π). This is the *torii*, an archaic structure that is most likely related to other types of portals such as the Chinese *p'ai-lu*, if not actually, as some scholars suggest, with the *torana* of ancient India.

The principal building of the inner shrine, the *naigu*, is reserved as the house of the "body" of the divinity, that is to say, the metal mirror, which as we have seen is one of the three imperial emblems transmitted by the sun goddess. The simplicity of an undecorated line contributes to the vision of a unified whole; where decorative detail is used, it contributes a note of concentrated beauty that relates organically to the effect of the building. Short hollowed-out decorations are added to the planks that finish the gables, and to other elements of the wood, which is left in its natural color throughout. The sanctuary at Ise, with its celebrations consisting of offerings and acts of purification, has from the beginning been the fulcrum point of the Japanese nation's political life. Every event that concerned the state or the institution of sovereignty was announced there to the sun goddess by a special messenger, who offered her in the name of the sovereign various gifts and rolls of silk as a token of thanks and tribute. The offering ceremony ended with an evocative ritual whose framework and setting was the austere simplicity of the place.

The fragility of the construction of such sanctuaries, which made use only of vegetable materials, made for the rapid corrosive action of time and bad weather, so that it was necessary to take measures that later became a ritual in themselves. Under the reign of the Emperor Temmu (A.D. 672–686) it was established that the sanctuary should be rebuilt, at alternate sites, every twenty years, the reconstruction to be modeled after the original sanctuary. This measure, respected

So, having been expelled, His-Swift-Impetuous-Male-Augustness descended to a place called Tori-kami at the head-waters of the River Hi in the Land of Idzumo. At this time some chopsticks came floating down the stream. So His-Swift-Impetuous-Male-Augustness, thinking that there must be people at the head-waters of the river, went up it in quest of them, when he came upon an old man and an old woman, — two of them, — who had a young girl between them, and were weeping. Then he deigned to ask: "Who are ye?"

So the old man replied, saying: "I am an Earthly Deity, child of the Deity Great-Mountain-Possessor. I am called by the name of Foot-Stroking-Elder, my wife is called by the name of Hand-Stroking-Elder, and my daughter is called by the name of Wondrous-Inada-Princess." Again he asked: "What is the cause of your crying?" The old man answered, saying: "I had originally eight young girls as daughters. But the eight-forked serpent of Koshi has come every year and devoured one, and it is now its time to come, wherefore we weep." Then he asked him: "What is its form like?" The old man answered, saying: "Its eyes are like *akakagachi*, it has one body with eight heads, and eight tails. Moreover on its body grows moss, and also chamaecyparis and cryptomerias. Its length extends over eight valleys and eight hills, and if one look at its belly, it is all constantly bloody and inflamed."

Then His-Swift-Impetuous-Male Augustness said to the old man: "If this be thy daughter, wilt thou offer her to me?" He replied, saying: "With reverence, but I know not thine august name." Then he replied, saying: I am elder brother to the Heaven-Shining-Great-August-Deity. So I have now descended from Heaven." Then the Deities Foot-Stroking Elder and Hand-Stroking-Elder said: "If that be so, with reverence will we offer her to thee." So His-Swift-Impetuous-Male-Augustness, at once taking and changing the young girl into a multitudinous and close-toothed comb which he stuck into his august hair-bunch, said to the Deities Foot-Stroking-Elder, and Hand- Stroking-Elder: "Do you distil some eight-fold refined liquor. Also make a fence round about, in that fence make eight gates, at each gate tie together eight platforms, on each platform put a liquorvat, and into each vat pour the eight-fold refined liquor, and wait." So as they waited after having thus prepared everything in accordance with his bidding, the eight-forked serpent came truly as the old man had said, and immediately dipped a head into each vat, and drank the liquor. Thereupon it was intoxicated with drinking, and all the heads lay down and slept. Then His-Swift-Impetuous-Male-Augustness drew the ten-grasp sabre, that was augustly girded on him, and cut the serpent in pieces, so that the River Hi flowed on changed into a river of blood. So when he cut the middle tail, the edge of his august sword broke. Then, thinking it strange, he thrust into and split the flesh with the point of his august sword and looked, and there was a sharp great sword within. So he took this great sword, and, thinking it a strange thing, he respectfully informed the Heaven-Shining-Great-August-Deity. This is the Herb-Quelling Great Sword.

Chamberlain: *Ko-ji-ki* (II edition, *pp*. 72–76)

Before this the two Gods Ama-terasu no Oho-kami and Yamoto no Oho-kuni-dama were worshipped together within the Emperor's Great Hall. He dreaded, however, the power of these Gods, and did not feel secure in their dwelling together. Therefore he entrusted Ama-terasu no Oho-kami to Toyo-suki-iri-bime no Mikoto to be worshipped at the village of Kasanuhi in Yamato, where he established the sacred enclosure of Shiki. Moreover, he entrusted Yamato-oho-kuni-dama no Kami to Nunaki-iri-bime no Mikoto to be worshipped. But Nunaki-iri-bime no Mikoto was bald and lean, and therefore unfit to perform the rites of worship. . . .

3rd month, 10th day. Ama-terasu no Oho-kami was taken from Toyo-suki-iri-hime no Mikoto, and entrusted to Yamato-hime no Mikoto. Now Yamato-hime no Mikoto sought for a place where she might enshrine the Great Goddess. So she proceeded to Sasahata in Uda. Then turning back from thence, she entered the land of Ōhomi, and went round eastwards to Mino, whence she arrived in the province of Ise.

Now Ama-terasu no Oho-kami instructed Yamato-hime no Mikoto, saying: — "The province of Ise, of the divine wind, is the land whither repair the waves from the eternal world, the successive waves. It is a secluded and pleasant land. In this land I wish to dwell." In compliance, therefore, with the instruction of the Great Goddess, a shrine was erected to her in the province of Ise. Accordingly an Abstinence Palace was built at Kaha-kami in Isuzu. This was called the palace of Iso. It was there that Ama-terasu no Oho-kami first descended from Heaven.

Aston: *Nihongi* (*pp.* 151–52, 176)

Following page:
17. Detail of the gables and roofs of the Izumo Shinto complex. Taisha-machi, Prefecture of Shimane.

over the centuries and extended to other sanctuaries, has allowed for the almost complete preservation of the primitive forms. This can be confirmed by comparing the present-day structures with the descriptions and drawings handed down by antiquity. The last construction of the Ise sanctuary took place in 1954.

Not all the sanctuaries undergo reconstruction every twenty years, however. The last reconstruction of the Izumo sanctuary, for example, dates back to 1744. It is thought that Izumo has handed down the most archaic type of Shinto cult edifice, with its characteristic central pillar. The eight columns set in the corners and at the halfway points of each side made it necessary to place the entrance with its external stairway not at the center, but on one side or the other of the central pillar. The shrine proper consists of a wooden building surrounded by a veranda with a balustrade. The planks at the two ends of the roof cross at the top, scissors-fashion (Fig. 17), but at Izumo they have lost their original function as a finish to the gable, and have been made into a crest for the building with a purely symbolic and decorative value. The same is true of the cylindrical blocks of wood set transversely on the ridge of the roof. The square plan of the edifice and the arrangement of the roofed entrance staircase at one end of the facade are other elements from the most ancient plans, which were later abandoned in favor of a rectangular edifice that has no central pillar and where the entrance is set at the center of the facade. The present-day sanctuary at Izumo includes some later elements, however, such as the treatment of the gable and the slightly curved roof.

This aspect of the shrine exemplifies the principal innovations that Shinto architecture later took on under the influence of Buddhist architecture of continental Asian — and basically Chinese — derivation. *Shinto* — that is, the "way of the gods" — had gathered together the indigenous beliefs and cults; later it merged with the Buddhist doctrine introduced from the continent, in a form of worship known as *ryobu-shinto* (the "*shinto* of two aspects"), which was reflected in the architectural field in the fusion of forms and decorative elements. On the whole, however, Shinto architecture preserved the simplicity of the most ancient forms and the essentially linear conception of their plans, with only slight structural differences even in the stylistic variants. These concerned for the most part the diverse arrangements of colonnades, the inclination and projection of the coverings, the setting of the entrances on the shorter or longer sides of the edifices, parallel or at right angles to the ridges of the roofs. The Shinto sanctuary, moreover, appears to have resolved from the beginning the principal structural problems of Japanese architecture. These of course remained closely connected with the material used, which was always wood: in the south, bamboo; in the center and north *hinoki*, a kind of cypress whose wood — of elegant grain and compact but easily worked fiber — is very resistant to atmospheric elements, so much so that it has survived in edifices over a thousand years old. Other vegetable materials used in the constructions were bark, rice straw, and the *miscanthus* (an Asian grass), used for the roof coverings. The use of vegetable materials in construction and the setting of the architecture within the landscape have remained through the centuries the basis of the immensely refined garden art of Japan.

THE ANCIENT CAPITALS

The Protohistoric Period

Up to the sixth and seventh centuries A.D. Japan lived in a protohistoric cultural setting. Far from remaining insular, however, she had entered the cultural sphere of China a long time before, partly through the mediation of Korea. Japan's Yayoi civilization had absorbed numerous elements of Chinese origin, bronze and iron objects that testify to the importance of influences and suggestions that had come to the archipelago from the superior civilization of the continent. From the third century B.C. on, China had followed a policy of expansion, which not only brought her colonizers to the outermost regions of present-day China, but pushed her troops from one side of the empire to the other, toward central Asia in the west, toward Manchuria and Korea in the east. In 108 B.C. the Emperor Wu of the Han dynasty established, in Korean territory, the prefecture of Lo-lang, which was the first of four colonies, or Chinese detachments, in the peninsula. The branch, extended out toward Japan from Korea, did not take long to bear fruit. News of the archipelago spread quickly in Lo-lang and other outposts of Chinese culture in Korea, at first by means of Japanese ships, and then, after the first century A.D., through diplomatic missions, which were registered in the Chinese chronicles of the time. Chinese sources record that already at the beginning of the Christian era Japan was made up of hundreds of little states or countries, formed most likely by the union of the various tribal or noble groups in the different parts of the land, which in turn followed the consolidation of the strongest clans into groups of a more developed state character. In the third century A.D., according to the same sources, the state of Yeh-ma-tai took the lead; probably situated in the northern districts of the island of Kyushu, it carried out an intense exchange of diplomatic missions with the continent.

The relationship between the Yeh-ma-tai of the Chinese sources and Yamato in central Japan has not yet been definitively established. In any case, Yamato was the grouping destined to unify the country, despite the resistance of several small states, such as Izumo, and clans, such as the Kumaso and the Emishi, who were remnants of the Japanese Neolithic populations. According to the oldest Japanese chronicles — *Kojiki* ("Memories of Antiquity") and *Nihon-shoki* ("Annals of Japan") — the national state was founded in 660 B.C. by Jimmu, grandson of a divinity descended from the goddess of the sun, who was supposed to have led an expedition to conquer Yamato. Although the story is legend, and has no precise historic basis, it does allude to certain circumstances in the political unification of the nation which are confirmed by archaeological data.

The funerary tumuli of the Kofun period characteristically represent the increased power of the large noble groups. Their construction also shows the forces already at the disposal of governmental units

CHINA'S DISCOVERY OF JAPAN
(Fifth Century A.D.)

The Wa dwell on mountainous islands southeast of Han [Korea] in the middle of the ocean, forming more than one hundred communities....

The women outnumber the men, and the men of importance have four or five spouses; the rest have two or three. The women are faithful and not jealous. There is no theft, and litigation is infrequent. When men break a law, their wives and children are confiscated; when the offense is serious, the offender's family is extirpated. At death mourning lasts for more than ten days, during which time members of the family weep and lament, without much drinking and eating; while their friends sing and dance. By baking bones, they practice divination, in order to ascertain their good or bad fortune. When they go on voyages, they appoint a man who is not allowed to comb his hair, to wash, to eat meat, nor to approach women. He is called the fortune keeper. If the trip proves propitious, they make him a valuable present; but if illness or misfortune overtake them, they deem that the fortune keeper was not scrupulous and unite in putting him to death....

During the reigns of Huan-ti (147–168) and Ling-ti (168–189), the country of Wa was in a state of great confusion, war and conflict raging on all sides. For a number of years, there was no ruler. Then a woman named Pimiko appeared. Remaining unmarried, she occupied herself with magic and sorcery and bewitched the populace. Thereupon they placed her where few people saw her. There was only one man who was in charge of her wardrobe and meals and acted as the medium of communication. She resided in a palace surrounded by towers and stockade, with the protection of armed guards. The laws and customs were strict and stern....

Four thousand *li* away to the south of the queen's land, the dwarfs' country is reached; its inhabitants are three to four feet in height. After a year's voyage by ship to the southeast of the dwarfs' country, one comes to the land of naked men and also to the country of black-teethed people; here our communication service ends.

Tsunoda: *Japan in the Chinese Dynastic Histories*

18. View of the western enclosure of the Horyuji. Inside, the five-story pagoda. Seventh and eighth centuries A.D. (Nara Period). Horyuji, Prefecture of Nara.

Following pages:

19. Colonnade of the western enclosure of the Horyuji, In the background (left) a view of the temple pagoda. Seventh and eighth centuries A.D. Horyuji, Prefecture of Nara.

of the time, which controlled vast territories and huge masses of men. The change that is seen in the funerary objects, in which armor and iron weapons suddenly dominate, points to the intrusion of armed groups into the peaceful agricultural areas of the Bronze Age. This ethnic superimposition, due to the immigration of nomadic groups coming first from the edge of the continental steppes and then from Manchuria and Korea, may have initiated the process of unification in Japan. Traditional historiography condenses these events in the legendary figure of Jimmu, who is supposed to have headed a campaign of conquest from Kyushu toward the north, subduing the populations of the southwestern and central regions of the archipelago and founding the Japanese empire. The expansion policy of the first period was not, however, limited to the archipelago. It was directed toward the Korean peninsula as well, and reflected an almost precocious historic vocation for continental expansionism.

The national legend includes the narrative of an expedition to Korea conducted by the legendary Empress Jingo against the state of Silla between A.D. 191 and 200. Korean sources say nothing of it, but they do speak of piratical Japanese incursions and then, in the fourth century, of wars by the Japanese against the states of Silla and Koguryo. These military campaigns led to the foundation, in the southern part of the Korean peninsula, of the Japanese protectorate of Mimana, which was lost in 562 because of Silla's domination in eastern Korea. It also seems that from the fourth century on the kingdom of Paekche, situated in the southwestern part of the peninsula, tried to establish friendly relations with Japan in order to defend itself against invasions by Silla and frequent frontier conflicts with Koguryo. In fact, Japan may have intervened in Korea against these two states just to defend Paekche.

The contacts with Paekche (called Kudara in Japanese annals) had a great impact on the civilization of the archipelago, since the role of cultural mediator, previously undertaken by the Chinese colony of Lo-lang, was now taken on by Paekche. Through Paekche the Japanese became acquainted not only with Chinese art, but more important with Chinese writing and Buddhism as well. At the beginning a large number of Koreans went to the archipelago; they taught the Chinese language and ideographic writing, the sciences, arts, and architecture. Entire communities of Koreans, followed by Chinese from Manchuria, moved in great numbers to the Japanese archipelago, so that by the middle of the sixth century there were over one hundred thousand immigrants, many of whom eventually assumed key posts in the social and economic life of the country.

In the field of thought, Taoism and Confucianism spread. The latter, based on the teaching of Confucius (551–479 B.C.), introduced the concept of ancestor worship as an expression of filial piety, and the concept of the just social order, which every individual in the state is required to uphold. Taoism (from *tao*, "the way") — dating from the legendary preaching of Lao Tzu and based above all on the works of Chuang Tzu (circa 369–285 B.C.) — cultivated belief in the active forces of nature, together with various forms of magic and divination arts, later merged in China into the so-called religious Taoism; the divination and magic eventually became part of Shinto as well.

From the middle of the sixth century on, Buddhism also penetrated Japan. From India, its place of origin, Buddhism had spread over the centuries to China and then to Korea before reaching the archipelago, where at first it met strong resistance from the indigenous cult of the *kami*, the gods of the Japanese naturalistic pantheon. At the time of the introduction of Buddhism, the native cult was a group whose mythology had strong political overtones, and was rapidly growing into a state religion. The continental stimulus of Taoism and Confucianism had provoked its growth in the historical period, so that the worship of natural and animal forces was flanked by the veneration for ancestors, above all for the sun goddess, progenitress of the imperial family.

20. Detail of the upper stories and spire of the eastern pagoda in the Yakushiji complex. Total height of the building: 131 feet. Seventh and eighth centuries A.D. Prefecture of Nara.

21. Detail of the head of the bronze statue of the Great Buddha (Daibutsu). Dating from A.D. 606, this statue is kept in the Asukadera at Nara, and is one of the first examples of Japanese Buddhist monumental sculpture.

Nara: Plan of the Yakushiji
1 *Southern gate* (nandaimon)
2 *Central gate* (chumon)
3 *Cloister* (horo)
4 *Golden Hall* (kondo)
5 *Hall of texts* (kyozo)
6 *Hall of the bell* (shoro)

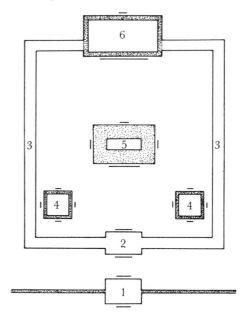

22. Detail from a bronze sculpture by Tori, depicting one of the Bodhisattvas of the Buddha Sakyamuni trinity. Height: 36.9 inches. Sculptured in A.D. 623. Horyuji, Nara.

23. Detail from the gilded bronze statue of the Buddha Bhaisajyaguru (Yakushi Nyorai), the Buddha of medicine. Height: 8 feet, 4 inches. Second half of the seventh century A.D. Yakushiji, Nara.

The priestly classes of the cult, the Nakatomi and Mononobe, waged a bitter struggle against Buddhism when it was first introduced. The Emperor Kinmei had placed Buddhism under the patrimony of the house of Soga, and the chancellor Soga no Iname set up, in his palace at Mukuhara, the first Buddhist chapel, the Mukuhara-dera. In it was placed the gold-plated bronze statue of Buddha given him in 552 by a Korean king. Some time later a raging pestilence was used by the Nakatomi and Mononobe (who spoke of the resentment of the local gods as its cause) as a pretext to have the new faith banished. But the pestilences and calamities ended by damaging the Nakatomi and Mononobe, and the Soga were able to return to profess their faith. By the middle of the seventh century Buddhism had triumphed, becoming the official state religion in Japan. The sympathy given to it, especially by the royal court, was undoubtedly related to the conviction that the new faith represented a vehicle of superior civilization, above all because of the magnificence of its architecture and art. The introduction of Buddhism marks the dividing line between "original" and "classical" Japan. However, the history of this event is still veiled by legend, since the first historic sources date from the seventh century A.D. and are very confusing and contradictory.

Together with the help of archaeology, however, these sources show the foundation of a unified state took place some time about the fourth century A.D. It was known as Yamato, from the name of that central region, which is now the modern district of Kinki. Because of its geographical position this territory had been strategically important from the beginning of Japanese political history, and recent discoveries indicate that the first imperial residence may have been established in the city of Naniwa, now a part of present-day Osaka. Historical tradition mentions the first palaces that the "emperors" Ojin (270–310?) and Nintoku (313–399) are supposed to have erected on the hill in Osaka, where in 1583 Toyotomi Hideyoshi undertook the construction of a huge castle. It was later destroyed and subsequently rebuilt by the Tokugawa in the first part of the eighteenth century. For centuries the district of Kinki remained the political and cultural center of the country; besides Osaka, Nara also was part of this center, and in the Asuka and Fugiwara areas on Nara's outskirts many imperial residences sprang up. Only toward the end of the eighth century did the region begin to lose its political importance, when a rather complicated series of circumstances necessitated a definitive transfer of the capital to the not-far-distant area of present-day Kyoto.

The centuries-old custom of Japanese political life was that every emperor, on ascending the throne, should establish his residence in a new site. The imperial palace was then built there and the site remained the nation's seat of government for the duration of the sovereign's reign. At times, however, the change of capital, or of the seat of the imperial residence, took place even during an emperor's reign. A partial consequence of this was the lack of a really thorough urban development until a permanent capital was established, although recent archaeological discoveries indicate that the places where the various imperial residence sprang up at the beginning of the eighth century show some development typical of a real capital. The Asuka area of Nara was particularly well developed, and its name is conventionally used to designate the period from the introduction of Buddhism to the foundation of Nara, in 710.

Introduction of Buddhism

Buddhism was officially introduced in Japan in A.D. 552. (According to some sources, the event came earlier, in 538.) It is no exaggeration to say that the event marked the beginning of a new era in the political and social life of Japan. In the wake of Buddhism, Chinese culture became so widespread that many of the old indigenous

24. **Figures of a humanoid sort. Detail from the sculptured decoration on the base of the statue of Yakushi Nyorai (Figure 23). Second half of the seventh century A.D. Yakushiji, Nara.**

Osaka: Reconstruction of the original nucleus of the Shitennoji

Osaka (ancient Naniwa), Plan of the Shitennoji complex
1 Southern gate
2 Central gate
3 Cloister
4 Pagoda (to)
5 Golden Hall
6 Reading hall (kodo)
7 Hall of texts
8 Hall of the bell
9 Pools
10 Secondary hall

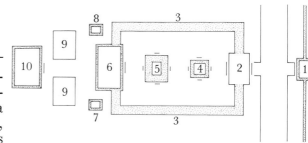

customs were completely abandoned. Emperors and their counselors began to deal directly with China, bypassing Korean mediation, and undertook the transformation of the court and the state, using the Chinese as their model. Together with the statesman Soga no Umako, the Empress Suiko (554–629) and the Prince Regent Shotoku Taishi (572–622) were the major figures in this process of the nation's reconstruction. According to tradition, in 604 Shotoku issued a code of moral edicts in which the Confucian and Buddhist experience were almost completely set above the indigenous tradition. The seventeen articles of the code indicated harmony as the basis of human life and of social existence; they held that in the civil organization the interests of the individual had to be sacrificed to the common interest, and that individual aspirations should not be set above the fulfillment of one's duties. The state was to be set up in a hierarchic form with the greatest powers in the hands of the sovereign. Obedience, honesty, self-control, diligence, sincerity, and loyalty were to be the bases of good government.

The Prince Regent Shotoku sent monks to China, promoted diplomatic and study missions, constructed numerous Buddhist temples. Many other religious structures were built at the expense of private individuals. As early as 624, there were forty-six Buddhist monasteries in the various provinces. In 692 no less than 545 monasteries and temples were functioning. Many of them no longer exist; others, such as the Shitennoji (the temple of the four celestial kings), have been completely rebuilt. The best preserved is the Horyuji, near present-day Nara, founded in 607 but rebuilt in 670 after a disastrous fire. Figure 18 shows the western enclosure of the temple, from which the roofs and spire of the pagoda emerge. The temple is the oldest existing example of wooden architecture in the world. The plan faithfully imitates that of the Chinese monasteries: a large rectangular cloister, with the main entrance portico to the south, encloses an open space in which are located the five-story pagoda and the pavilion called the *kondo* (golden hall), containing the Buddha image and other works of art and worship. Behind these is a building used for the reading of sacred texts that is flanked by smaller edifices used for the library and the great bell. The cloister, covered by a jutting roof, has a monumental central gate of four bays: the two at the center form the entranceway, and two side ones are filled by the statues of the protector kings.

The golden hall (*kondo*) and the pagoda in the Horyuji are set on the same transverse line, but in the Shitennoji the pagoda was built on the longitudinal axis of the courtyard, hiding the *kondo* from view at the entrance. The *kondo* in the Horyuji is a low rectangular pavilion set on a stone platform, from which rise twenty-eight pillars that support the upper part of the structure and form four bays on one side and five on the other. The elaborate roof has curved eaves. The columns of the temple have a slight entasis, that is, a slight swelling in the center (perhaps of distant western derivation) and are set into low stone bases (Figure 19). They do not have capitals but hold up a series of brackets and are connected with one another by means of a regular system of beams. In China only stone or brick pagodas have survived from this epoch, and these do not faithfully reproduce the wooden pagodas. The building type is the equivalent of the Indian *stupa*, the Buddhist reliquary inspired by the funerary tumulus, and is normally developed on a square plan, with a central pole, whose top consists of small bronze circles, the symbolic equivalent of the parasols which top the *stupa*. The floors decrease in size: in the Horyuji, the four lower floors have three bays on each side, the fifth has two; the roof, like that of the other edifices, has curved eaves.

The pagoda is certainly the most characteristic structure in Buddhist architecture, the one that has the greatest height and elevation of its stories. Many pagodas are limited to three floors, however, as is the case with the Yakushiji pagoda, almost 131 feet high, erected between the end of the seventh and the beginning of the eighth century. Figure

20 shows a partial view of the top floor of this pagoda, the roof, and the tall spire with its metal circles. Over the ages the traditional idea has not altered nor has the building type changed. This conservatism has been favored by the very nature of the monument, which, as a reliquary, is considered a closed structure. The upper floors, even in their organic unity, have no problems with the articulation of interior space. Totally nonfunctional, they bear only a symbolic and decorative value, as does the tall spire with its metal rings or laminated flame.

Figurative art also embraced the themes of Buddhism. The new faith had brought the worship of images to Japan, and the temples abounded in statues of Buddha and Bodhisattvas. Five categories of spiritual beings had already been developed by Chinese iconography and were transplanted to Japan. First of all were the images of the historic Buddha, Sakyamuni, ideally portrayed in monastic garb with the signs (*laksana*) that distinguish the sacredness of his person: the *usnisa*, the protuberance of the cranium, is the symbol of perfect knowledge, the long ear lobes express the great hearing faculty, the lens-like *ulna* in the middle of the forehead is a sign of spiritual election. The *mudra*, the ritual hand gestures in the different body poses, express the various moments and aspects of Buddha that iconography commemorates and the piety of worship venerates. Images of the historic Buddha were later flanked by those of the metaphysical Buddha in his diverse personifications: the Bhaisajyaguru, the Buddha of medicine (in Japanese, Yakushi); Maitreya, the Buddha of the future (Miroku in Japanese); and many others that reflect the infinite aspects that the incommensurable superhuman dimension of Buddha can assume.

The Bodhisattvas were the second iconographic category; these celebrated the spiritual beings who, although they have attained the "essence of illumination" (which is the literal meaning of *bodhisattva*), postpone for an indefinite period losing themselves in *nirvana*, in order to follow the vocation of dedicating themselves to the salvation of all creatures. Buddhist iconography depicts them therefore with a worldly aspect, evident in the sumptuousness of their dress and the preciousness of the jewels they wear. Contrasted with them were the *arhat*, those personages of lofty spirituality who, through meditation and the careful observation of Buddha's precepts, have attained illumination and have chosen to be extinguished in *nirvana*. Of this iconographic category, T'ang dynasty (618–907), Chinese art began to celebrate those *arhat* who, like the Bodhisattvas, were able to renounce *nirvana* in order to stay on the earth and protect Buddhist law. But the most strenuous task of defending the faith was assumed by another category of beings, the *deva* (celestial kings), hardy and inflexible guardians of the law, whose terrifying and pitiless aspect expresses the zeal with which they attend to their duty of repelling the assaults of the evil spirits. Images of winged beings, celestial nymphs, and mythical animals make up the last iconographic category, to which, in the gradual process of humanizing the faith, portraits of the patriarchs and the most illustrious masters of Buddhism were added.

During its initial flourishing, the Japanese iconographic repertory was still closely linked to the Chinese and Korean types. The first sacred images came from Korea. A wooden statue of Bodhisattva Avalokitesvara (in Japanese, Kannon Bosatsu) is known as the Kudara Kannon since it was thought that it was imported from Paekche (Kudara in Japanese) in Korea. King Songmyong of Paekche is reputed to have sent the first statue of Buddha to Japan with a recommendation to introduce Buddhism into Japan. According to the *Nihon-shoki* the letter that he sent to the Yamato court of Japan in 552, reads: "The doctrine is excellent, the most excellent, but it is difficult to penetrate and explain: not even a king of the Chou dynasty or Confucius could attain such perfect knowledge. It assures unlimited and incommensurable happiness, virtue and fortune, and leads to the supreme illumination. From distant India to the Three Han (Korea) there is not a spirit who does not cultivate this doctrine, and

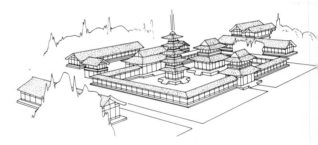

Nara: Reconstruction of the original Horyuji complex

Nara: Plan of the central complex of the Horyuji. The original placement of the buildings according to the layout of the seventh century. To the right, the present-day arrangement.

1 Central gate
2 Cloister
3 Pagoda
4 Golden Hall
5 Reading hall
6 Hall of texts
7 Hall of the bell

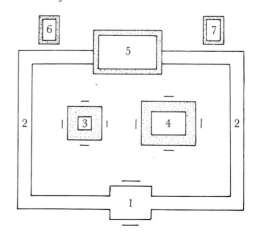

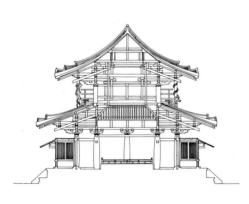

Nara: Transverse section of the golden hall of the Horyuji

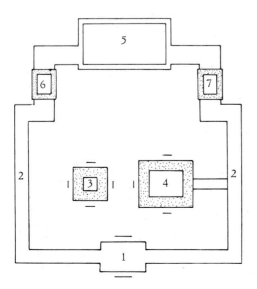

for this reason, I, Songmyong, king of Paekche and your vassal, send you my emissary with respect so that you may spread it in your empire. . . . Buddha, in fact, said: 'My law will spread towards the East.' "

Buddhist Influences on Japanese Art

Other gifts of statues and sacred writings came from Korea in the second half of the sixth century. Sources say that in 577 there was another tribute from Paekche of statues and books, as well as architects and a sculptor; another statue arrived two years later, and two more in 584. In the meantime the Korean artists and artisans — and only in the following generation the Japanese themselves — established and spread the canons of the new images of worship. Thanks to Korean mediation, Buddhist art arrived in the forms of the Chinese Six Dynasties (420–589) style, in particular the Buddhist art of the northern Wei dynasty (386–534), which had easily and quickly spread to the Korean peninsula. Wei dynasty art had effected the transplantation of Buddhist art to China and had given new local accents to Indian and central Asian iconographic forms. In the northern rock temples, which had risen at Yun-kang, Lung-men, and Tun-huang, like those situated along the caravan tracks of central Asia, sculpture and painting had marked the initial stages of stylistic progression. From strict adherence to Indian and central Asian prototypes they grew, little by little, to have an autonomous creative language that took into account even the bodily peculiarities of the Far Eastern man, while still retaining rigorous respect for the basic iconographic canons.

Japanese sculptural production in the first period is directly connected with China's Yun-kang and Lung-men art in certain respects, although there are differences, imposed above all by the use of different materials. In Japan stone statuary was unusual. Wood and bronze (often gilded) were the only substitute materials, at least up to the time when lacquer sculpture became widespread. It is therefore useless to look for the monumentality and heavy structure of stone statuary in Japan. Some works — such as the bronze head (Figure 21) which is the only part left of the great statue of Buddha of Asuka-dera (A.D. 606) — strive to reproduce the colossal forms of Chinese sculpture. Bronze, cast with the lost wax molding technique, has much greater plasticity than stone, so the effect of hieratic rigidity that stone gives to statuary was lost. Moreover, in its necessarily more moderate dimensions, Japanese sculpture usually avoids any facile monumentality in order to create figures in which the grace of the limbs and the sweetness of the faces register as more than elements of experiment or analysis. The modeling was also less frontal than that of the prototypes. An example of this is the Shaka Triad (Shaka Sanzon), one of the first masterpieces of Japanese Buddhist sculpture, depicting Buddha Sakyamuni flanked by two Bodhisattvas in the form of servants. The detail in Figure 22 is one of the two Bodhisattva figures. Even in the perhaps exaggerated photographic setting, it shows an image of absorbed serenity whose contained, archaic smile is no longer a stylistic convention but rather the mark of palpitating humanity. The work, with an inscription on the back of the halo dating it in 623 and attributing it to Tori Busshi or Kuratsu-kuirbe no Tori, is kept in the Horyuji. It fully demonstrates and acknowledges the artistic dignity of sculpture, which on the continent of Asia had enjoyed only the rank of a minor art.

The inscriptions on the statue form the first important documents on Chinese writing in Japan and are a source of precious historical references. For example, from the epigraph it is known that the Shaka Triad was commissioned by the wife and sons of Prince Shotoku during his last illness. The custom of erecting temples and statues as vows or votive offerings to effect the cure of illustrious personages exemplifies the message of hope that Buddhism represented. Another statue, the Triad of Yakushi Nyorai, or Buddha Bhaisajyaguru (Figure 23) flanked by the Bodhisattvas Gakko and Nikko (not seen in the photograph), is related to the iconography of another work preserved in the Horyuji at Nara, whose inscription mentions the vow made by the Emperor Yomei (about 519–587). Ardently trusting in being cured of an illness, the emperor had ordered the erection of a temple and a statue in honor of the Buddha of medicine. He died before being able to see the work completed; it was then probably completed in 607 by the Empress Suiko and his (Yomei's) son Shotoku. If such is the case, the inscription is probably apocryphal, since it is doubtful that a cult of Yakushi Nyorai existed at the end of the sixth and beginning of the seventh centuries in Japan. Moreover, on stylistic and technical bases as well, the first and second statues of the work in the Horyuji seem to be, respectively, from the second half, and from the beginning, of the seventh century. Nonetheless, it is interesting to note the votive meaning the inscription contains, since it is similar to the sort of meaning given to a large part of the Buddhist statuary of the time.

The Yakushi illustrated in this volume, seated cross-legged and dressed in a monastic cloak, is considered the masterpiece of all Asian Buddhist sculpture for the purity of its features, the proportions of its limbs, and the fluidity of movement of its dress. Even the base of this statue is a unique piece of sculptural decoration, containing reliefs of classical motifs and animal-like figures of uncertain symbolism (Figure 24). It is difficult to find other examples of these in Japan, and because of their very exceptional nature some scholars have thought that this is an imported work. It has been suggested that the figures derive from certain gnomes in Indian art and express a primitive state of nature in subhuman form, over which Buddha's law allegorically comes to reign. They would thus be symbols of the power of faith, which reaches not only all men but all other beings as well. In any case, the iconography, totally extraneous to Japanese art, can be used to document the vast range of influences that the Japan of the time absorbed.

Other indications of these Chinese contributions come from the wooden masks, which often represent western physical types, with unequivocally non-Mongoloid features. The specimen in Figure 25 is an exception, since it depicts a Chinese personage of princely rank, whose exploits may have been the basis of a court dance that was introduced in Japan in the first half of the seventh century, from China or Korea, together with the entire repertory of spectacles called *gigaku*. However, even the figurative stereotype of this mask recalls, with its long ear lobes and prominent nose, central Asian or Indian rather than Chinese iconography, even if it does essentially respect Buddhist canons. Other masks, whose plainly Indo-Persian profiles approach caricature or the grotesque, can be assumed to represent the thoroughly international climate of Japan at the time: a reflection of the contemporary Chinese cosmopolitanism, but also a sign of the open attitude of the Japanese toward continental life.

It is worth noting that the same figure who stands out in seventh-century Japanese history, Shotoku Taishi, appeared even in his own time as the emblematic synthesis of a long process of material and spiritual development, with its roots in the most remote parts of Asia. Some have even spoken of the presence of Christianity as an influence at the dawn of Japanese history. Shotoku Taishi is presented by historic tradition as the man who is born in a stall, bearing superhuman signs of predestination. His patronage of a new faith was such that he can at least be defined as the Constantine of Japanese Buddhism. Such hagiography does not obscure his virtues as an enlightened statesman, however. On the contrary, by presenting him as the *vir novus*, it symbolically epitomizes in him a large part of the political and social revival of the seventh century. The reforms of the Taika era that followed (645–649) were most likely inspired by him or by

25. Theatrical mask of the *gigaku* type, representing a Chinese prince from the state of Wu. Painted wood; height, 11.33 inches; width, 8.33 inches. Seventh century A.D. (Asuka Period). From the treasury in the Horyuji. (Tokyo National Museum).

Following pages:
26. Aerial view of part of the residential area of the ancient city of Heijo-kyo (present-day Nara), founded in A.D. 710. Note the geometric regularity of the plan.

his work, and led to the old noble order gradually yielding its place to a bureaucratic state that sanctioned the principle of state property over individual or tribal rights. Once this was accepted, Japan was able to adopt the administrative system in force in China during the T'ang dynasty (618–907). The principal objective of the Great Reforms of the Taika period was the strengthening of the central power, obtained by means of a division of the land into provinces, whose administration was given over to government functionaries. At the same time a new agrarian reform and taxation system were adopted. The numerous innovations, which must have radically modified the structures of ancient Japan, were gathered together in a lengthy code, the *Taiho-ritsuryo* of 701, which at least in theory has provided the basis for every subsequent legal and administrative code in Japan.

Nara

In the meantime, following the establishment of relations with China, a thoroughly non-provincial culture spread over the country. Chinese scholars and technical experts flowed into the archipelago and introduced a real transplant of Chinese culture in Japan. In 710 a permanent capital was established, on the site of the present-day city of Nara. It was called Heijo-kyo (The Capital of Peace); an aerial view of part of its ruins can be seen in Figure 26. Its rectangular plan, the chessboard layout of building blocks, the imperial palace and the government buildings set up in the north-central sector of the city, were all modeled after Ch'ang-an, capital of the Chinese Sui (581–618) and T'ang (618–907) dynasties. The city was built within an area 2.17 miles east-west by 2.44 miles north-south. The buildings of the imperial palace were arranged in a vast enclosure surrounded by a boundary wall. The principal artery began from the center of the palace enclosure and ran north to south, cleaving the city in half, similar to the practice in Chinese cities. Such plans show a knowledge of Roman town-planning, which had come down to China together with other contributions of the classical Western world.

Like the town-planning, the architecture also took its forms from the Chinese models; the architecture of the Chinese palace of the T'ang period was the prototype of the luxurious new dwellings of the nobility. Plans called for buildings to be disposed according to criteria of strict symmetry and set around a central open space, which was used as a garden. The principal building, the residence of the head of the family, was oriented to the south and connected to the minor residential buildings by means of corridors with verandas reached through portals. The great patriarchal family was polygamous, and required large residences for all the various members of the family, concubines, and servants.

The new metropolis was the most evident expression in Japan of a civilization oriented toward the continental world: architecture and arts were Chinese; the dress and etiquette of the courtesans and functionaries were Chinese; the official language and writing were Chinese. A brilliant court aristocracy, profoundly imbued with Chinese ideas, grew up. Even the administration of public life progressively emphasized its Chinese derivation. New schools of learning taught Confucian doctrine and were used to form the ranks of a new bureaucracy chosen from among the nobles. The consolidation of the imperial institution was effected along the lines of Chinese ideology and official Chinese historiography, even though the ways of legitimizing power were sought in purely local tradition, rather than in the "will of heaven" the Chinese used as a justification for the emperor's power. In Japan the emperor's descent from the sun goddess justified his rule.

The *Kojiki* and the *Nihon-shoki*, compiled at the beginning of the eighth century, were the first works that sanctioned the principles of the descent and divine nature of the imperial institution on the basis of national legend. With these works the literary history of the archi-

IMPERIAL EDICT FOR THE FOUNDATION OF THE CITY OF HEIJO (NARA)

The Princes and Ministers all say: From olden times till the present day it is an imperative act of statecraft to make the foundations of the Palace by calculating the day and by observing the stars, to build the Emperor's Capital after obtaining the date through divination, and by observing the site, thereby making the foundations for establishing the seat of government lasting and strong.

Since their feelings are so sincere, it is difficult to oppose their counsel. Moreover, the Capital being the residence of the officials, the place where people from everywhere come together, this is a matter for rejoicing, not for Us alone, and since it is profitable, how could We be opposed to it? ...

Now this site of Heijo (Nara) is in harmony with the four cardinal points protected by three mountains, divination with the turtle and the sticks has yielded similar favourable results; therefore the Capital ought to be built, the cost of construction ought to be reported entirely in accordance with the real conditions. Further, roads and bridges ought to be built after the autumn harvest has been reaped. Do not let the workers become too exhausted, be systematic, so that afterwards additions are not necessary.

Snellen: *Nihongi* IV

Nara: Plan of the Kofukuji complex, according to the original arrangement of A.D. 710.

1 *Southern gate*
2 *Central gate*
3 *Cloister*
4 *Principal golden hall*
5 *Hall of texts*
6 *Hall of the bell*
7 *Reading hall*
8 *Dormitories*
9 *Eastern golden hall*
10 *Western golden hall*
11 *Pagoda*
12, 13 *Octagonal pavilions* (nanendo, hokuendo)

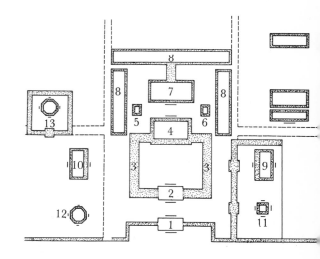

27. Meditation and prayer hall of the Kofukuji complex, known as the *hokuendo* or octagonal pavilion. A.D. 721 (Nara Period). Kofukuji, Nara.

pelago also took shape. The attempt already made by the *Kojiki* to adapt Chinese ideographic writing to the Japanese language was more felicitously carried out in the *Manyoshu* ("The Collection of Ten Thousand Leaves"). This anthology of thousands of poems celebrated love, nature, the gods, the pleasures and agonies of life; in it, emperors, poets, and humble soldiers rubbed shoulders. It was the first monument of Japanese poetry and represented the most genuine parts of what had been preserved from the ancient traditions of life and thought in the archipelago. Yet by the time the *Manyoshu* was compiled, continental culture had already permeated every sector of Japanese society and customs. In 747 the Emperor Shomu (701–756) decreed that in every province a Buddhist monastery and a convent should be built at the state treasury's expense. The need for a numerous clergy distributed throughout the nation began to be

felt; this not only favored the spread of Buddhist religion, it favored cultural growth as well, since the temples functioned also as schools and study centers, besides rendering the service to noble families of directing their younger sons toward a religious life. The edict of Shomu, set into motion at once, caused a great increase in architectural activity and the almost immediate development of culture and the arts.

In Buddhist architecture the new Chinese influence was somewhat tempered by the architectural tradition already established in the preceding period. The city of Nara remained the center of this new religious architecture for centuries. Subject to constant continental influence, the architects of Nara experimented with solutions that revealed indisputable originality, transforming the Chinese models, which were almost all of stone, into structures of wood which were lighter in structure and more organic in their proportions. Many monasteries were moved to the new city, and others were built there: the Yakushiji monastery, founded in 681, was transferred to Nara

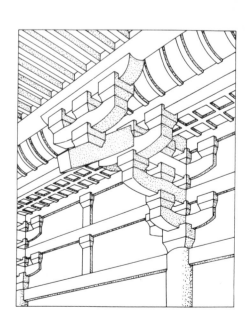

29

Opposite:
28. Facade of the major building in the Toshodaiji complex, the *kondo*, or golden hall. The principal images of the temple are kept here. The ground floor measures 91 feet 10 inches by 48 feet. Circa A.D. 760 (Nara Period). Prefecture of Nara.

29. The Daibutsuden, or Hall of the Great Buddha, in the Todaiji complex at Nara. Originally built in the eighth century A.D. to house a monumental statue of the Buddha, it was the largest wood construction in the world. Destroyed by fire in A.D. 1180, together with other temple edifices, it was later rebuilt on a smaller scale. The latest reconstruction dates from A.D. 1709.

Brackets and beams of the Toshodaiji golden hall.

in 718. The Kofukuji was begun in Nara in 710 at the expense of the powerful Fujiwara family. The octagonal pavilion (*hokuendo*) in Figure 27 is one of the original structures of this epoch, and has its later equivalent in the *yumedono* (hall of dreams) of the Horyuji, built in the place where Shotoku Taishi was supposed to have meditated. The *hokuendo* was built in 721 in the northwestern area of the temple grounds and was until that time a building type unknown in Japan. It was made up of an octagonal pavilion surrounded by a cloister and was used as a private chapel for the offering of prayers for the benefit of the founder of the temple.

Between 755 and 770 the construction of the Toshodaiji was begun; this was founded by Chien-chen (688–763), a Chinese monk known under the name of Ganjin, who had been called by the Japanese clergy to reestablish the correct Buddhist discipline. The new temple offered a renewed synthesis of Chinese and Japanese structural and stylistic elements, with a tendency toward the majestic, and simple but rather static and heavy forms. Among the original structures of the Toshodaiji the reading hall and the golden hall (*kondo*) remain. The former, which is in any case the oldest reading hall in existence, was probably originally a hall of Heijo-kyo's imperial palace used for official meetings and later given to the temple by the emperor and adapted to the needs of the monastery. The *kondo* (Figure 28), dates from about 760. This building, which has seven bays on one axis and four on the other, has many elements in common with the residential architecture of the period, and probably perpetuates the formal and imposing models of the T'ang style Chinese palaces. In both Japan and China religious architecture seems to have differed little from civic architecture, particularly the residential architecture of the court. Certain buildings in the imperial palace complexes had a ceremonial function similar to that of the temples, and so possessed a corresponding sacredness. The imperial rank was, after all, considered a terrestrial reflection of celestial supremacy and then, with Buddhism, identified with an emanation of the metaphysical Buddha.

The most grandiose architectural achievement of the period was the Todaiji (the Great Temple of the East), the most important site of Buddhist worship in Japan, built entirely at the expense of the treasury at the behest of the Emperor Shomu (701–756) and the empress, who, when they lost their son at a tender age, had sought comfort in the faith. The exaggerated religiosity of the imperial couple had great consequences. It furnished the impetus for architecture and religious art, at their peak during the so-called Tenpyo periods (724–748). In its original form, which was destroyed by fire in 1180, the Todaiji seems to have been flanked by two large seven-story pagodas, each of which formed a complex in itself, with a cloister and four lateral gates. Between them was the golden hall, enclosed in turn in a large cloister that communicated to the north with the residences of the monks. These consisted of a dormitory, which was then joined to the reading hall by means of a veranda, which was also connected to the refectory. Most of the edifices have disappeared: the rebuilt golden hall is greatly reduced in size, compared to the original, and like many other structures, it is a relatively modern reconstruction.

The temple had been erected under imperial patronage to house the Daibutsu (the Great Buddha), a colossal statue that had been offered up to exorcise the plague and other calamities that had swept over the country from 737 on. In the preceding year, the Hua-yen sect had been introduced from China; this was founded by Tu-shun (557–640), who was known in the archipelago as Kegon, and had spread the faith of the Universal Vairocana Buddha (in Japanese, Roshana), of whom all the other Buddhas, including Sakyamuni, the historical Buddha, are manifestations. The Daibutsu was the most monumental sculptural work of the period, almost fifty-three feet high and weighing almost 550 tons. After many attempts it was finally cast in pieces, then soldered and gilded by an expert of Korean origin called Kuninaka no Kimimaro. Over 500 pounds of gold were needed for the gilding work; this was furnished by a mine that was discovered almost miraculously for the occasion. The huge dimensions of the statue give a clear idea of the technical progress Japan had made up to this time. The pavilion that housed the statue was the largest wood construction ever realized in the world, covering an area of 244 feet by 168 feet, and over 118 feet high. The present-day pavilion (Figure 29), although imposing — it is still the largest wooden building in the world under one roof — is about half the size of the original. The present-day Daibutsu statue, which is a mediocre seventeenth-century reconstruction, is also much smaller than its original. In 752, at the sumptuous inauguration ceremony of the statue, called "the eye-opening," Japan suddenly became the center of East Asian Buddhism. Diplomatic missions came from as far away as Indochina and India. They came out of their devotion to Buddha, but also as an implicit act of tribute to the Emperor Shomu, who could by then proclaim himself the Vicar of Roshana on earth.

30. Wood statue of Yakushi Nyorai, the Buddha of medicine. Height: 5 feet 6.8 inches. Circa A.D. 793 (Nara-Heian Period). Jingoji, Kyoto.

31. Shukongo-shin, the lightning bearer, one of the protective gods of Buddhism. Height: 6 feet 8.5 inches. Detail of the bust. Circa A.D. 733 (Nara Period). Sangatsudo, Todaiji, Nara.

IMPERIAL PROCLAMATION ON THE ERECTION OF THE GREAT BUDDHA IMAGE OF THE TODAIJI

On the fifteenth day of the tenth month of the fifteenth year of the Tempyo reign [743] . . .

We take this occasion to proclaim Our great vow of erecting an image of Lochana Buddha in gold and copper. We wish to make the utmost use of the nation's resources of metal in the casting of this image, and also to level off the high hill on which the great edifice is to be raised, so that the entire land may be joined with Us in the fellowship of Buddhism and enjoy in common the advantages which this undertaking affords to the attainment of Buddhahood.

It is We who possess the wealth of the land; it is We who possess all power in the land. With this wealth and power at Our command, We have resolved to create this venerable object of worship. The task would appear to be an easy one, and yet a lack of sufficient forethought on Our part might result in the people's being put to great trouble in vain, for the Buddha's heart would never be touched if, in the process, calumny, and bitterness were provoked which led unwittingly to crime and sin.

Therefore all who join in the fellowship of this undertaking must be sincerely pious in order to obtain its great blessings, and they must daily pay homage to Lochana Buddha, so that with constant devotion each may proceed to the creation of Lochana Buddha. If there are some desirous of helping in the construction of this image, though they have no more to offer than a twig or handful of dirt, they should be permitted to do so. The provincial and county authorities are not to disturb and harass the people by making arbitrary demands on them in the name of this project. This is to be proclaimed far and wide so that all may understand Our intentions in the matter.

Tsunoda *et al: Sources* (Vol I, *pp.* 104–105)

Arts of the Nara Period

In the other Buddhist centers as well there was a considerable development of the figurative arts. Already around 700 the Horyuji had been adorned with mural paintings, of which those in the *kondo* (which survived up to the tragic fire in 1949) represented the Buddha of infinite Light, Amitabha (Amida in Japanese), surrounded by his celestial court and by numerous standing and seated Bodhisattvas, in a pictorial style harking back to the Indian frescoes at Ajanta and those in the central Asiatic rock temples. The collaboration established with Chinese artists and the deepening knowledge of the new religion enlarged the iconographic repertory to include, besides the figures of Buddha and Bodhisattva, those of the minor divinities and the apostles of the faith.

In sculpture, clay and lacquer were added to the already existing mediums of bronze and wood. Lacquer sculpture, called *kanshitsu* (dry lacquer), was a technique of Chinese origin. It consisted of wrapping layers of cloth soaked in resin around roughly cut figures of clay, wood, or straw. The lacquering gave consistency to the cloth and made it possible to mold it while it was still wet. When the lacquered cloth dried, the internal form could be removed, leaving a light and hollow statue, which was easily carried in processions. Because of its high cost, however, due to the value of the raw materials (particularly the lacquer), this type of sculpture never became widely diffused and clay statuary, tempered with straw or paper fiber or with mica, was often substituted for it. The outer surfaces were then covered, as were lacquer or wooden statues, with gold leaf, gold paint, or some other varnish. Among the most noteworthy examples of the sculpture of this period is the wooden statue of the Yakushi Nyorai of the Jingoji temple at Kyoto (Figure 30), which dates from the last years of the eighth century and is one of the first standing images of the Buddha of medicine. The work, sculptured from one block of cypress wood, was left in its natural state, except for light coloring given to the eyes and lips.

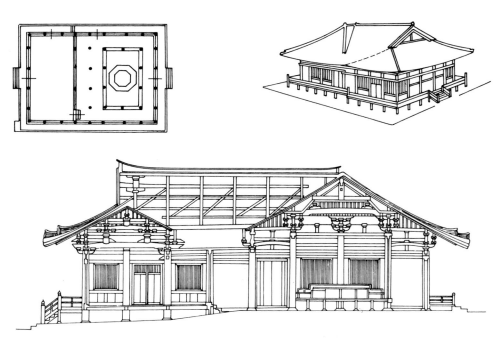

Nara: Plan, elevation and transverse section of the Todaiji hokkedo.

32. **Shosoin** (storehouse) of the Todaiji. This building houses the collection of imperial art donated to the temple in A.D. 756 on the death of the Emperor Shomu. Dimensions of the base: 109 feet by 31 feet; height: 45 feet 9 inches. Eighth century A.D. (Nara Period).

The rather heavy volumes of the dress and forms reveal an Indian influence.

Thematically the group of statues of the guardian kings of the law in the Todaiji — related to the clay effigies of the Shukongo-shin (Vajrapani in Sanskrit), one of which is illustrated in Figure 31 — is also famous. The image of the "thunderbolt-bearer" expresses, with a certain rigidity of movement, the terrific ardor with which this demon defends the law. Executed, according to tradition, in 733 for the Kinshoji, it was then brought to the *sangatsudo*, a building of the Todaiji. The flashing expression and terrifying aspect of this statue gave rise to the belief that it could come to life. Tradition states that during the course of a civil war it transformed itself into a hornet and subdued the rebels. Because of its miraculous powers it was considered one of the secret images and sealed up in a reliquary, which was opened only once a year in a solemn ceremony. The fact that it has been rarely exposed accounts for its well-preserved rich original polychrome.

Stylistically the sculpture of this period harks back once again to Chinese Buddhist iconography, but many works are already indisputably Japanese, in both their formal and their figurative conception. The portraiture is plainly Japanese in aspect, and though it offers only images of religious personages in conventional poses and Buddhist masters seated in rigid attitudes before their disciples, it foreshadows the development of a portrait art which has no peer in all Asia. Sculpture did not deal only with religious subjects, however. A genre of no little artistic importance was the mask. These were sculptured in wood with extraordinary realism and often with a sharp sense of caricature. The variety of subjects, often non-Japanese, indirectly reflects the curious position of the Nara court in relation to every expression of overseas tradition, though the masks were later accepted in the repertory of indigenous spectacles, both profane and religious. The genre also demonstrates the high level reached by the secular arts, development of which was assured through the employment of artists and artisans by the state. A specially created office or department had four masters, sixty painters, twenty sculptors, twenty potters and twenty lacquerers in its employ. Their works were naturally meant for the imperial court. Other artists worked for the temples, and also lent their talent to civil works. The monk Gyoki (688–749), one of the most eminent of the time, was not only the Emperor Shomu's spiritual teacher, but he planned roads, bridges, dams, and ports, and seems even to have designed the first map of Japan.

The impetus given to the arts — to metallurgy, weaving, lacquering and other artisan techniques — naturally required larger resources of valuable raw materials, especially gold and silver. The mining firms intensified their search for these materials, and profited from the demand. At the beginning of the eighth century, the first coins — imitations of those from China, which had been in circulation since A.D. 699 in the archipelago, after the discovery of copper deposits — were put into circulation. The monetary economy did not flourish, however, because the finer metals were reserved for the making of ceremonial and religious objects for the court and the temples. Many of these objects have been preserved in temples of a particular type called *shosoin* (storehouses), which were also used as archives for the transaction and records of public offices, and for manuscripts and other valuable works. The *shosoin* were elevated buildings without windows, made of tree trunks cut lengthwise into poles of triangular shape and set horizontally one on top of the other, forming a very compact and closed structure. The result not only met the needs of security but also guaranteed the best preservation of the works stored there. The building system took advantage of the natural characteristics of wood. The wood shrank in dry weather, thus allowing for ventilation, and expanded in wet weather, preventing air and moisture from entering.

The most important *shosoin* was the one built in 756 in honor of the Emperor Shomu within the enclosure of the Todaiji (Figure 32).

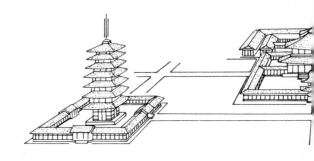

Nara: Reconstruction of the Todaiji complex.

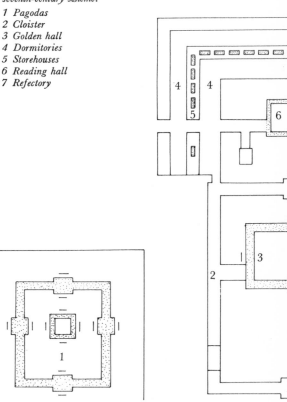

Nara: Plan of the Todaiji according to the original seventh-century scheme.

1 *Pagodas*
2 *Cloister*
3 *Golden hall*
4 *Dormitories*
5 *Storehouses*
6 *Reading hall*
7 *Refectory*

TANKA POETRY

Rather than worry
Without result,
One should put down
A cup of rough *sake*.
If I revel
In this present life,
In the life to come
I may well be a bird,
May well be an insect.
"All creatures that live
In the end shall die."
Well, then, while I live
It's pleasure for me.
Otomo No Tabito (665–731) in Bownas & Thwaite: *Japanese Verse* (*pp. 32–34*)

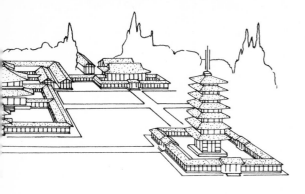

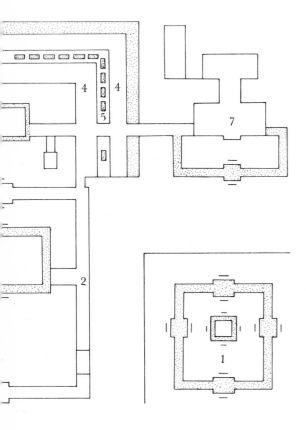

Following page:

33. Toshodaiji: Detail from the corner of the building used as a storehouse for sacred texts. Note the elegant crossing of the wooden poles. Eighth century A.D. (Nara Period). Prefecture of Nara.

Consisting of two stories, it is one of the biggest of its time and the only one surviving from the Nara period. The treasure contains a unique collection of Japanese art objects, dating for the most part from the Nara age, as well as art pieces that testify to the importance given to contacts with the Asian continent during this period. The nucleus of the collection consists of the personal objects of the Emperor Shomu; forty-nine days after his death, the empress donated these things to the Todaiji. Other objects come from donations made in 752 by nobles, provincial temples, or foreigners visiting or living in Japan at the time. There are objects from China, India, Persia, besides those made in Japan in continental styles. Commercial and trade products are kept on one side; on the other side are the works of state artisans: brocades, bronze and gold vases, lacquered work, and glass and mother-of-pearl objects that testify to relations with the Roman-Syrian world through China. Equally well known are the *sutras* deposited in the Toshodaiji (Figure 33 shows the crosswork of the wooden poles of this edifice).

As Buddhism grew in power, it unfortunately became a menace in Japanese politics. The network of temples built for the protection of the land demonstrated that Buddhism had entered civil life, and was as a religion able to defend the country both from calamities and from the forces of evil. The first aspects of Buddhism to gain a hold were those in which the most important element was the immediate protection offered by Buddha and the Bodhisattvas — from the miracle worker Yakushi and the merciful Kannon, to the Shitenno, the staunch defenders of the faith. Varying interpretations of the sacred scriptures and their recitation for the good of the state, gave rise to various schools of worship. These were the seven sects of Nara, and none lost time in attempting to conquer the temporal power. A monk named Dokyo (died 772), favored by the Empress Koken (born 718), aspired to the throne; his attempt was the manifest sign that the imperial house was beginning to lose its authority and prestige. Yet the lack of a precise rule of succession, which purposely left the throne open to any of the children or their kin, to avoid as much as possible any threat to the dynasty, also fomented internal discord.

Influential noble families in the court sphere were often able to acquire control of funds, which properly belonged to the state. And important changes made in the *Taiho-ritsuryo* affected the handling of money and property in such a way as to drain even further power from the emperor: the progressive increase in population, and the lack of sufficient cultivable land, led in 703 to a plan for the exploitation of uncultivated land, with the concession of the profits of large lots for three generations to those who cultivated them. In 743 a law guaranteed the perpetual possession of such land to the almost exclusive benefit of the clergy and nobility, so that after only a century the principle of state property had already been seriously compromised and impaired. The Chinese administrative system revealed its weaknesses in a country like Japan, where there were no provincial cities to guarantee the efficiency of a central government and where the relatively small population (six million) was not really a strong rural pressure and influence. The utmost liberty of action was thus left to those who wanted to take over land holdings. Threats to the state by a clerical class that had become more and more involved in the affairs of temporal power, and by an aristocracy thirsty for wealth — both groups centered in the capital — led to the failure of Nara's political mission and made a transfer of the government to a new region of the nation necessary in 748.

THE GOLDEN AGE

Kyoto

The Emperor Kammu (737–806), one of the last great rulers of ancient Japan, made the decision, in 784, to move the capital from Nara to Nagaoka, the place that the oracles and geomancers indicated as the most suitable for the construction of the new imperial palace. In order to accomplish such a move, the state had to bear a heavy financial burden, not only for the construction of new buildings but for indemnities on the moving expenses of the court nobility. But the proximity of the intriguing Buddhist clergy at Nara made the transfer all but impossible to avoid.

During the next ten years construction on the new city went ahead; three hundred thousand workmen were employed. The imperial palace and the government offices were completed in a few months, and the court was soon installed, but construction of roads and communication links was still going on when, in 793, because of a series of calamities and unlucky circumstances that had struck the city under construction, Kammu decided that the work should be suspended and that the capital should be built in another locality! This time consultations with the diviners indicated the region of Yamashiro, and thus in 794 the foundations were laid for Heian-kyo (The Capital of Peace and Tranquility), the city that was to be known later as Kyoto, or Miyako (the capital) and which was to remain the imperial residence until 1867. The new city was unable, even from its beginnings, to elude religious influence, particularly Buddhist influence. It was soon under the protection of the four genii of the cardinal points, and of a temple, the Enryakuji, which was built on the summit of the nearby Mount Hiei. The conditions for Kyoto becoming a second Nara were germinating. It seemed to matter little that, to obtain a better defense of the city, a large clay statue of a warrior, armed with bow and arrows and wearing a helmet and cuirass, was ritually buried on a hill east of the capital. When the capital or the empire was menaced, legend has it that a sad chant came from the warrior's tomb. It was often not enough to save the day.

Kyoto was situated in a privileged position. Nara, surrounded by a mountain range, had always been difficult of access, but Kyoto was at the same time placed in the center of the country and connected to the coast by means of the Kamogawa river. This river, connected in turn with the Yodogawa, was a direct line of communication with Osaka, already the most important maritime emporium in Japan. The plan of Kyoto varied little from Nara's, or, for that matter, from the plan of Ch'ang-an in China. Kyoto was much larger than Nara, however, and in its architecture — its palaces, temples, and residences — the first really original Japanese solutions were worked out. Built on a rectangular area measuring roughly three and one-quarter miles by two and nine-tenth miles, with the shorter sides facing north and

34. Byodoin: View from above of the complex of the Hoodo, or Phoenix Hall. A.D. 1053 (Heian Period). Prefecture of Kyoto.

south, it was cut by large parallel and perpendicular roads, running north to south and east to west, giving a pattern of large rectangular blocks. A wall with a double moat surrounded it. At the center of the northern side, on a plot 17,945 square yards in area, the imperial buildings, with their attached complex of offices and residences, were erected. From the palace compound exit a large artery ran north to south dividing the city into two administrative units, the "right capital" and the "left capital," ending at the Rasho Gate (Rashomon), which was the main urban entranceway.

Heian-kyo was destined to become the center of a new culture. By the time of its founding, Chinese culture had been thoroughly assimilated in Japan, and there now grew up a profound national consciousness, a thoroughly Japanese spirit, which was to find its literary and artistic expression in the life of the new city.

The architecture was a courtly classicism of severe forms that, though inspired by Chinese building types, was tempered by local taste and by suggestions from the stylistic solutions already worked out in Japan by Buddhist architecture. The edifices of the imperial palace were a rather monumental reworking of pure Japanese native style, built of

34

wood, with wood flooring and roofs covered with *hinoki* bark. Edifices such as the Shinsenin, one of the imperial buildings, laid the foundation for the style of aristocratic houses called *shinden*. In such houses symmetrical organization of the building into two wings left ample space in the central courtyard for a garden. But unlike the garden-park that the Shinto sanctuaries and Buddhist temples kept in as natural a state as possible, the gardens of these residences were elaborate miniature compositions that, through careful respect for proportions, achieved an effect of space and variety typical of a much larger natural landscape. This miniature garden was often a garden-lake, made up of a pool from whose water emerged rocks, which symbolized islets and were connected to the shore by little wooden or stone bridges.

A manual of garden art written in the thirteenth century by Tachibana Toshitsuna, entitled *Sakuteiki*, describes the *shinden*-style gardens in minute detail. This type of garden lay at the basis of the later evolution of the art, conceived to harmonize architecture with the countryside, uniting man's work with the work of nature by means of the harmonious combination of two distinct orders of compositional elements, the first botanical (flowers, young trees, shrubs), the second tectonic (hills, rocks, pools, waterways). In the Nara epoch, the lake with its rocks had already taken on the symbolic identity of the oriental sea, with the mythical islands in which Chinese Taoist legend had placed the land of the blessed, where the drug of immortality grew.

Among the few surviving examples of residential architecture from this period is the Hoodo of the Byodoin (Figure 34 gives a panoramic view). The complex is without a doubt one of the most elegant and refined compositions in all Japanese architecture. It is situated in a picturesque natural setting, in the valley of the Uji river, in a locality between Nara and Kyoto in which imperial residences had previously been built. The initial nucleus of constructions had been erected by Fujiwara Michinaga (966–1027). In the middle of the eleventh century, his son, Yorimichi (922–1074) built the Byodoin there, according to the custom of the nobility of the time of dedicating small temples in their own residences for the prestige of their family and as a token of religious piety. The Hoodo, the only complex saved from fires, is set on the bank of a small lake (Figure 36), whose limpid water, reflecting the buildings, heightens the effect of a splendid, fabulous architecture, the embodiment on earth of the magnificence of the Buddhist paradise. Known as "The Pavilion of the Phoenix" (Hoodo), because of a gold-plated bronze phoenix set on the roof of one of the buildings, it develops according to a plan that symbolizes this mythical bird, which in Japan had become a symbol of prosperity and peace. The central hall is its body, the two side arcades that end in two square pavilions are the wings, and the elongated rear hall is the tail. The linking of the structures, and their form, are a precious record of Heian period architecture. The roofs — here still made of tiles according to the ancient Chinese custom — break up, with their diversity of levels, forms, and protuberances, the uniformity and monotony of the facades of the one-story structures.

Other important specimens of Heian architecture are to be found in various isolated temple buildings that preserve the forms of residential architecture. Figure 35 illustrates the twelfth-century quadrangular pavilion or great hall of Fukidera. It is a simple structure with large squared pillars, which recall the sober and humble aspect of ancient provincial dwellings. Only the roof has a really monumental effect; it is covered with tiles, unlike the one in the Kyoto Sanzenin (Figure 37), approximately contemporary, which is covered by a thick layer of *hinoki* bark, according to the pre-Buddhist custom maintained in rural dwellings and Shinto sanctuaries. During the Heian period such roofs were applied to aristocratic residences more and more often, effecting a further merger of architectural work with nature. On the other hand, the golden hall of the Joruriji (Figure 38), is of more classical inspiration, practically reechoing the architectural models of the Nara period. Figures 40–41 show modern reconstructions of two edifices, the Gotaido

35. Fukidera: The Great Hall. Built on a
quadrangular plan, with a large, jutting
roof. Twelfth century A.D. (Heian Period).
Prefecture of Oita.

Opposite:

36. Byodoin: View of the lake garden and part of the Hoodo complex. A.D. 1053 (Heian Period). Prefecture of Kyoto.

37. Sanzenin. Principal building of the temple, with a roof of vegetable fiber. A.D. 1148 (Heian Period). Prefecture of Kyoto.

38. Joruriji: Facade of the entrance to the golden hall. Twelfth century A.D. Prefecture of Nara.

Following pages:

39. Joruriji: Partial view of the temple pagoda. A.D. 1178 (Heian Period). Prefecture of Nara.

40. Daigakuji: Gotaido. Modern reconstruction of a ninth-century A.D. building. Prefecture of Kyoto.

41. Daigakuji. Shoshinden. Fourteenth-century A.D. (Momoyama Period) reconstruction of a Heian Period edifice. Prefecture of Kyoto.

38

41

and the Shoshinden of Daigakuji, a temple originally founded in the ninth century, so it is impossible to specify the innovations effected over the centuries. But these structures are counted among the first in Japan that expressed the search for forms independent from those of China.

Growth of a National Culture

The gradual detachment from continental architecture was at a certain point determined and in part speeded by the interruption of Japan's relations with China. The Chinese influence remained conspicuous in the imperial court and aristocratic spheres, yet it was not long before even these were feeling the need for a cultural renewal and greater autonomy. With the fall of China's great T'ang empire in 907, the Japanese realized that the country that had been their model for centuries was not without its weaknesses and shortcomings. Before the dynasty's fall, however, relations with China had already been broken in 894, when Sugawara no Michizane (845–903) presented a petition to the throne dissuading the emperor from sending further missions to China. Not only was the political situation in China critical at the time, with the country lacerated by internal discord and peasants' revolts (the city of Ch'ang-an, which for centuries had been the inspiration and ideal of the Japanese, had been razed), but other motives justified such a decision: the Chinese missions were a heavy economic burden on the Japanese, and their usefulness had increasingly been compromised. They no longer served precise commercial interests, since Chinese merchants had set up regular bases in the Kyushu ports.

The Japanese had begun to be touchy, too, about the difficulty of establishing official relations with the "celestial empire" on a level of equality, thanks to the incurable Chinese attitude of considering all foreign missions as dutiful expressions of tribute and vassalage. In an epoch in which Japan had arrogated imperial dignity to itself, this state of affairs seemed unacceptable, creating a subtle feeling of irritation toward China, a reflection of which can perhaps be found in an eleventh-century literary work, the *Hamamatsu Chunagon Monogatari* ("Story of the Counsellor of Hamamatsu"). It tells the story of a Japanese politician who goes to China, gets the empress to fall in love with him, and gives her a child, which he does not hesitate to bring back to Japan with him. China takes on the symbolic role of an abandoned lover.

Politically speaking, Japan now felt mature enough to issue new edicts: Public administration was reorganized, yet the move brought little benefit to the state. In fact, any further decentralization of power it brought about was detrimental, if anything, to the imperial authority. The noble families profited by the edicts; their economic force had increased little by little with their growing control of vast land holdings, which were exempt from taxes. By custom these possessions became hereditary, and in the eleventh century they totaled almost half of the nation's territory. This brought on growing economic difficulties for the state and some internal disorder, while the provinces bettered their conditions, thanks to wise land policies and to the opening of roads and waterways for the transport of merchandise from the most remote territories to the landowners, who often lived in the capital, if not in the court itself.

The most powerful of the noble houses was the Fujiwara. Divided into various collateral branches, they dominated the situation of the government. Intent above all on gaining a stronger foothold in the imperial family by means of marriages, the political policy of the family was increasingly effective. From the ninth to the eleventh century the Fujiwara monopolized the highest state posts and were the power behind the throne. The principle of deputyship, or regency, which they effected, remained the political principle of Japanese government until modern times. The emperors attempted to weaken the Fujiwaras' power, but the only method they could devise was the extreme measure of claustral government, in which the emperor abdicated in favor of his son while the son was still a minor. The emperor then became a monk, carrying out his political activity from the sanctuary of a monastery, as a sort of emperor emeritus, forming a real government with its own independent court.

The institution of claustral government, established in 1086 and destined to last for seventy years, aimed at depriving the Fujiwara of authority little by little. It ended, however, by extinguishing what small prestige was left to the throne, since it divided those faithful to the imperial institution into at least two factions: the one made up of the followers of the monk-emperor, the other of those who sided with the emperor on the throne. In the meantime the Fujiwara nobles held power *de facto*. It is easy to imagine, given this state of affairs, the desperation of the intrigues and the weakness of any state authority backed by such varied claims to legitimacy. The flowering Heian civilization thus rested on shaky foundations, but it was kept alive by the splendor and prestige of the noble families of the court, above all the Fujiwara, and achieved its glory under Fujiwara Michinaga (966–1027), whose will was law, as regent and prime minister, for thirty years, from 995 to 1027, the apex of the epoch's culture.

The breaking off of relations with China had by this time led to independence in all cultural forms. In the religious field the Buddhist sects of the Nara period had given way to the Tendai and Shingon doctrinal sects. These were of Chinese derivation but had taken on totally Japanese characteristics. Their triumph was basically due to their magical and ritual character rather than the religious dogma they propounded. The ancient Shinto religion also underwent profound changes. From the fusion of Shinto and Buddhism a new faith was born, the so-called *ryobu-shinto* or "shinto of the double aspect." In it the Japanese gods were interpreted as incarnations or manifestations of the Buddhist ones. The goddess of the sun, Amaterasu, was considered the Japanese manifestation of Dainichi (Great Sun), the Universal Vairocana Buddha or Roshana. The theory was put forward by the monk Gyoki in 742, and developed to the point that the *kami*, the Shinto divinities, were considered the traces or marks left by the Buddhas and the Bodhisattvas, who were seen as having abandoned their original state (*honji*). The explicit formulation of the *honji-suijaku* was the basis of *ryobu-shinto*. Shinto and Buddhist places of worship were often unified and principles of faith with both Shinto and Buddhist characteristics were formulated.

This syncretism also involved the sacred arts. A Shinto iconography developed under the influence of Buddhism; nor did the architecture of the sanctuaries remain insensitive to the fascination of Buddhist architecture. A fusion of forms and decorative elements — among them metal trimmings totally foreign to the older Shinto structures — took place. On the whole, however, the austere simplicity of the older forms and the essentially linear concept of their plans were not lost. The stylistic variants were distinguished by the different arrangement of the colonnades, the inclination and projection of the coverings, the arrangement of the entrances on the short or long sides of the buildings, parallel or at right angles to the lines of the roof. The wood was colored red or vermilion, the beam-work and the ridges were curved and the eaves supported by ever more complex and elaborate brackets.

The sanctuary of Hachiman at Tsurugaoka, in the prefecture of Kanagawa, which dates from the twelfth century (Figure 42), might even appear to be a good example of continental Asian architecture, with its high pavilion roofs and the curved structures that make up the central cornices of some of its buildings. One of the usual building types of late Shinto architecture, it was the model for many later constructions, which rarely attempted new stylistic solutions. Made up of two groups of buildings, joined by a central structure that serves as a connecting element, it has a double entranceway on sides parallel

42. Hachimangu: Shinto sanctuary of Hachiman, the god of war. The temple complex shows the marked influence of Chinese architecture. A.D. 1180 (Heian Period). Tsurugaoka, Prefecture of Kanagawa.

SAICHO'S VOW OF UNINTERRUPTED STUDY OF THE LOTUS SUTRA

The disciple of Buddha and student of the One Vehicle [name and court rank to be filled in] this day respectfully affirms before the Three Treasures that the saintly Emperor Kammu, on behalf of Japan and as a manifestation of his unconditional compassion, established the Lotus Sect and had the *Lotus Sutra*, its commentary, and the essays on "Concentration and Insight," copied and bound, together with hundreds of other volumes, and installed them in the seven great temples. Constantly did he promote the Single and Only Vehicle, and he united all the people so that they might ride together in the ox-cart of Mahayana to the ultimate destination, enlightenment. Every year festivals of the *Golden Light Sutra* were held to protect the state. He selected twelve students, and established a seminary on top of Mt. Hiei, where the *Tripitaka*, the ritual implements, and the sacred images were enshrined. These treasures he considered the guardian of the Law and its champion during the great night of ignorance.

It was for this reason that on the fifteenth day of the second moon of 809 Saicho with a few members of the same faith, established the uninterrupted study of the *Sutra of the Lotus of the Wonderful Law*.

I vow that, as long as heaven endures and earth lasts, to the most distant term of the future, this study will continue without the intermission of a single day, at the rate of one volume every two days. Thus the doctrine of universal enlightenment will be preserved forever, and spread throughout Japan, to the farthest confines. May all attain to Buddhahood!

Tsunoda *et al: Sources* (Vol I, *pp.* 124–25)

43. Statue of a Shinto divinity; detail of the bust. The headdress and costume mirror the fashions of Japanese nobility of the time. First half of the ninth century A.D. (Heian Period). Kyoogokokuji, Kyoto.

FROM THE DIARIES OF COURT LADIES

Many months had passed in lamenting her lost world of love, more shadowy than a dream. Already the tenth day of the Deutzia month was over. A deeper shade lay under the trees and the grass on the embankment was greener. These changes, unnoticed by any, seemed beautiful to her, and while musing upon them a man stepped lightly along behind the hedge. She was idly curious, but when he came towards her she recognized the page of the late prince. He came at a sorrowful moment, so she said, "Is your coming not long delayed? To talk over the past was inclined." "Would it not have been presuming? — Forgive me — In mountain temples have been worshipping. To be without ties is sad, so wishing to take service again I went to Prince Sochino-miya."

"Excellent! that Prince is very elegant and is known to me. He cannot be as of yore?" [i.e. unmarried.] So she said, and he replied, "No, but he is very gracious. He asked me whether I ever visit you nowadays — 'Yes, I do,' said I; then, breaking off this branch of tachibana flowers, His Highness replied, 'Give this to her, [see] how she will take it.' The Prince had in mind the old poem:

The scent of tachibana flowers in May
Recalls the perfumed sleeves of him who
is no longer here.

So I have come — what shall I say to him?"

It was embarrassing to return an oral message through the page, and the Prince had not written; discontented, yet wishing to make some response, she wrote a poem and gave it to the page:

That scent, indeed, brings memories
But rather, to be reminded of that other,
Would hear the cuckoo's voice.

Izumi Shikibu

Having no excellence within myself, I have passed my days without making any special impression on any one. Especially the fact that I have no man who will look out for my future makes me comfortless. I do not wish to bury myself in dreariness. Is it because of my worldly mind that I feel lonely? On moonlight nights in autumn, when I am hopelessly sad, I often go out on the balcony and gaze dreamily at the moon. It makes me think of days gone by. People say that it is dangerous to look at the moon in solitude, but something impels me, and sitting a little withdrawn I muse there. In the wind-cooled evening I play on the koto, though others may not care to hear it. I fear that my playing betrays the sorrow which becomes more intense, and I become disgusted with myself — so foolish and miserable am I.

Murasaki Shikibu
Omori: *Diaries* (*pp.* 132, 149–50)

44. Onjoji: View from above of the temple complex, which is set into the landscape. A.D. 859–877 (Heian Period). Prefecture of Shiga.

with the roof line. The new sanctuaries were modified in general composition as well. The number of auxiliary buildings increased, the complexes were made larger, and Buddhist pagodas and pavilions even rose up in the enclosures. The interior halls began to house icons rather than the traditional sacred emblems. Not only were statues of Shinto gods sculptured, but there were statues of humans whom legend and history deified as brilliant examples of wisdom, holiness, or heroism. Ancestor worship was another source of inspiration for the Shinto of the historical age. The Shinto divinity depicted in Figure 43 is one of the oldest iconographic works of the religion, dating back to the first half of the ninth century. From the first examples of the genre, there is an amazing, profoundly national characterization of physical types and costume. Buddhism here had only a suggestive influence; it did not change the figurative canons either from the structural or stylistic point of view. Despite its tendency to syncretism, however, Shinto seems to have acquired even greater awareness of the national peculiarities of its cult, from which derives the plainly "Japanese" treatment of the subjects, sumptuously dressed according to court fashions.

45. Seisuiji: Access stairway to the temple, which rises on the slopes of a wooded hill. (Heian Period). Prefecture of Shimane.

Renewal of Buddhism and Its Architecture

Buddhist art during the Heian period was also renewed by the new aesthetic canons, and Buddhism itself took on new life with the introduction of new doctrines from China, which broke the monopoly of the seven Nara sects and progressively deprived them of authority. Saicho (767–822), venerated after his death as Dengyo Daishi, (the great master who transmitted the teaching), had studied in China the T'ien-tai (Tendai in Japanese) doctrine, named after the mountains on which the monk Chih K'ai (531–597) had erected a monastery; the monastery had become the center of the "Great Vehicle" school of Buddhism, based on the authority of the *lotus sutra of the good law* (the *Sutra* being one of the discourses of Buddha). Asserting the fundamental unity of all beings in the eternal and absolute nature of the Buddha, of which the historical Buddha (Sakyamuni) represented a temporary manifestation, the doctrine preached an ideal of the ascetic life of meditation, maintaining that the goal of salvation could be reached only by following, with absolute faith, the way Buddha had shown by his example. Dengyo Daishi transplanted this doctrine to Japan and established its center in the Enryakuji, mentioned earlier, a monastery whose construction he supervised personally, on Mount Hiei north of the capital.

The ascetic ideal of life was shared by the Shingon sect, which was founded at approximately the same time as Tendai, by Kukai, or Kobo Daishi (744–835), in the solitary monastery of Kongobuji on Mount Koya, south of the capital. Shingon (true word) is the Japanese pronunciation of the Chinese term Chen-yen (the doctrine of the hymns), the magic formulas in which the elements and essence of the universe were concentrated. Known in China also under the name of Mi-tsung (the school of the mysteries), it is a form of Tantrism, the ritualistic doctrine introduced from India in the eighth century, which is based on a "cosmo-theistic-magical" conception of life. In Shingon doctrine the universe is identified with the Buddha of the Great Light, who has a double aspect: absolute and static in the sphere of eternal, immutable ideas (the "adamantine world"); dynamic in the world of contingent phenomena, where he takes on the forms of gods, men, animals, and plants. Even the most humble being is a manifestation of Buddha, as is man in his totality, since his thought reflects the cosmic faculty, his words express its language. His body represents merely the phenomenal element. By practicing the three mysteries of the body, the word, and thought, man can unite with the Buddha. The symbolic ritualism of the Shingon sect derives from

KI NO TSURAYUKI
ON JAPANESE POETRY

Japanese poetry has for its seed the human heart, and grows into countless leaves of words. In this life many things touch men: they seek then to express their feelings by images drawn from what they see or hear. Who among men does not compose poetry on hearing the song of the nightingale among the flowers, or the cries of the frog who lives in the water? Poetry it is which, without effort, moves heaven and earth, and stirs to pity the invisible demons and gods; which makes sweet the ties between men and women; and which can comfort the hearts of fierce warriors. Keene: *Japanese Literature, An Introduction* (*p. 22*)

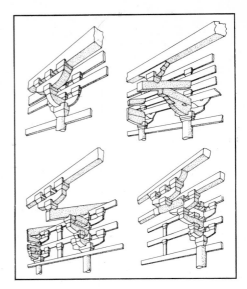

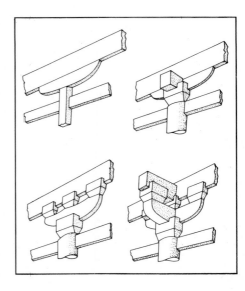

Simple and composite types of bracket supports, seen in their gradual development from the Asuka Period to the epoch of Kamakura.

46. Muroji: Five-story pagoda. Height: 53 feet 2 inches; base: 8 feet 2 inches square. The small dimensions of this pagoda and of the other pavilions of the temple are due to the limited amount of suitable building space on the plateau where the temple was built. Second half of the eighth century or beginning of the ninth century A.D. Prefecture of Nara.

47. Daigoji: Detail from the beams and bracket system of the five-story pagoda. Height of the building: 125 feet 4.5 inches. A.D. 951 (Heian Period). Kyoto.

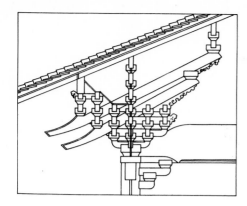

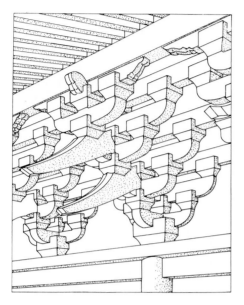

Simple and composite types of bracket supports, seen in their gradual development from the Asuka Period to the epoch of Kamakura.

48. Daigoji: The beams and brackets of the various floors of the pagoda. Kyoto.

Following pages:

49. Chusonji: Detail from the brackets in the golden hall covered with gilded sheets of metal A.D. 1124 (Heian Period). Hiraizumi, Prefecture of Iwate.

this conception; it prescribes positions, body and hand movements, and the recitation of sacred formulas.

Both the Tendai and Shingon doctrines, in the period of their transplantation in Japan, aroused the fervor of the primitive Buddhist communities. Their ideals of hermitage favored the construction of monasteries as well, no longer in the cities but rather in the elevated solitude of the mountains. Abandonment of the flat urban areas for the steep mountain slopes gave rise to the characteristic irregular arrangement of the buildings in the new monasteries and brought about the definitive renunciation of rigid Chinese ideas of symmetry — which, in fact, even China had had to abandon in building similar mountain temples. This general structural and stylistic reevaluation led to the search for a more organic placement of architectural works in their natural surroundings. This principle of natural setting marked the second period of evolution for Buddhist architecture in Japan, following the assimilation and evocative mixture of continental forms with indigenous techniques. The first mountain monasteries had risen in the Nara period, on heights south of the Yamato plain. The necessarily different plan of the buildings had imposed wide-ranging modifications in building technique, to achieve both a dynamic articulation of space and a lightening of load and stress. Together with the Enryakuji, the Kongobuji on Mount Koya was one of the principal monasteries of the period, and served as a model for later ones. The buildings of the complex, scattered over the forest, are almost literally united with nature, and borrow a great deal from the traditional simplicity of Shinto architecture.

The panoramic view of Onjoji, (Figure 44) illustrates the main characteristics of these mountain temples. Built in the second half of the ninth century, the entire Onjoji complex, both buildings for worship and dwellings, is set in the greenery. Figure 45 is a view of the access to Seisuiji, a monastery in the prefecture of Shimane; a gently graded stairway rises up the slope of a natural park. The Muroji, a temple founded by a monk from Kofukuji in an isolated spot in the prefecture of Nara, is distinguished by the free arrangement of its edifices according to the characteristics of the terrain. The pagoda and the golden hall are among the original constructions. Their relatively small size is due to the limits of available flat terrain. The five-story pagoda (Figure 46) shows the polychrome effect of the heightened tonalities of the wood and the red and golden decorative elements, in contrast with the plain white of the walls. The pillars of the pagoda have a slight convexity (entasis) and the beams supporting the roofs still possess the solidity of the Nara period; however, the roofs with their simple hard lines are no longer covered with tiles, but with a thick, very smooth layer of *hinoki* bark, according to the custom of traditional Shinto architecture. The pagoda no longer has eaves as such; the impetus of the structure is entrusted almost exclusively to the brackets, which often achieve considerable compositional complexity.

Figure 47 shows some details of the five-story pagoda of the Daigoji, a temple founded in 874 on a mountain southeast of the capital. The pagoda, built in 951, is 125 feet high and is one of the tallest in Japan. The spire makes up a third of the total height. The structural elements of the building can be taken as a good example of the support systems utilized by Japanese architecture to obtain an equilibrium of forces between horizontal and vertical structures, and to allow for a greater load and stress capacity on the pillars. The brackets, set between pillars and beams in order to decrease the stress on the latter, are perhaps the most noteworthy structural element in Japanese architecture. They are applied according to a variety of systems, combined in a more or less composite manner — like arms or chandeliers, etc. — and normally have a sort of boat form. They are connected to the pillars by means of capitals made of square blocks. In their more complex forms, such as in the illustrated examples, they extend not only longitudinally and transversely, but also vertically, interlocking

in series to correspond with the various levels where support for the intermediate reinforcement beams is needed. Figure 48 illustrates a sequence of a composite type bracket system and shows another characteristic of Japanese architecture: the treatment of all the elements as external structures visible from both inside and outside the edifice, according to an aesthetic totally unknown to brickwork building.

Figure 49 shows a detail from the interior of the golden hall of the Chusonji, the brackets and beams covered with gold leaf, their ends decorated in fretwork; this temple-mausoleum, built in the twelfth century in honor of Amida Buddha by Fugiwara Kiyohira, was then used to house the remains of Kiyohira himself and some of his successors, who were interred in the three altars in this golden hall. An even more striking decorative effect is illustrated in Figures 50 and 51, which show the union, in the same temple building, of gold and silver lamination with a decoration of the brackets by lacquer and inlays of mother-of-pearl, culminating in the ornamental "celebration" of the coffered roof decorated with arabesque designs. The total effect of an entire temple room is seen in the picture (Figure 52) of the golden hall of the Jingoji, on the slopes of Mount Takao at Kyoto, with the vivid, jarring contrast of the gold and black lacquering of the furnishings, the red of the pillars, the brackets, and the ceiling, and the white on the small spaces of the wall.

50. Chusonji: Arabesque decorations on the ceiling of the golden hall. A.D. 1124 (Heian Period). Hiraizumi, Prefecture of Iwate.

51. Chusonji: Detail from the woodwork of the golden hall, showing the gilded metal covering and metal fretwork of the brackets and beams. A.D. 1124 (Heian Period). Hiraizumi, Prefecture of Iwate.

52. Jingoji: Furnishings in the golden hall.
(Heian Period). Kyoto.

The altar decoration of the golden hall of the Chusonji (Figure 53) is another example of the affected elegance of the furnishings during the late Heian age, with embossed and inlay work in arabesques suggesting work of the Occident. The serpent-devouring king-peacock (*kujaku-myoo*), depicted with exquisite craftsmanship in the middle of the medallion, was deified by esoteric Buddhism as one of the "great kings," defender of the law from the evil spirits, and alleviator of natural calamities. The Shingon doctrine spread the cult of the peacock in Japan, linking its origins to a miracle: in 908, the monk Seiho was supposed to have prayed for rain in front of an image of this divinity that was set in the imperial palace garden, until the long drought came to an end. Behind this legend lies a contrasting, more ancient Indian belief. According to the Indian legend, in a former

53

53. Chusonji: The king-peacock. Detail from the altar decoration in the golden hall. A.D. 1124 (Heian Period). Hiraizumi, Prefecture of Iwate.

life Buddha was incarnated as a peacock and succeeded in this disguise in making miraculous water gush out of a fountain. The affected elegance of the Japanese composition (executed with a taste perhaps transmitted across the steppes from Moslem art) is a representative example of most of the ornamental arts of the Heian epoch. The importance Shingon attached to the execution of rites, the use of incense, chants, music, lights, and rich decorations, gave great impetus to such work.

54. Godai Kokuzo: The five manifestations of the Bodhisattva of infinite virtue. Height, 38 inches. Middle of the ninth century A.D. (Heian Period). Jingoji, Kyoto.

55. Byodoin: The Hoodo. Mural painting depicting the paradise of the Pure Land. A.D. 1053 (Heian Period). Kyoto.

56. Amida Nyorai, the Buddha of unlimited virtue. Gilded wood sculpture, the
work of Jocho (died A.D. 1057). Height, 9
feet 4 inches. Eleventh century A.D. (Heian
Period). Byodoin, Prefecture of Kyoto.

**FROM GENSHIN'S
"ESSENTIALS OF SALVATION"**

When a good man dies, earth and water depart
first, and as they leave gently, they cause no
pain. How much less painful then must be the
death of a man who has accumulated merit
through *nembutsu!* The man who carries this
teaching firmly in his mind for a long time
feels a great rejoicing arise within him at the
approach of death. Because of his great vow,
Amida Nyorai, accompanied by many bodhisattvas and hundreds of thousands of monks,
appears before the dying man's eyes, exuding a
great light of radiant brilliance. And at this
time the great compassionate Kanzeon extending hands adorned with the hundred
blessings and offering a jeweled lotus throne,
appears before the faithful. The Bodhisattva
Seishi and his retinue of numberless saints
chant hymns and at the same time extend their
hands and accept him among them. At this
time the faithful one, seeing these wonders
before his eyes, feels rejoicing within his heart
and feels at peace as though he were entering
upon meditation. Let us know then, that at the
moment that death comes, though it be in a
hut of grass, the faithful one finds himself
seated upon a lotus throne. Following behind
Amida Buddha amid the throng of bodhisattvas, in a moment's time he achieves birth in the
Western Paradise. . . .

Tsunoda *et al: Sources* (*p.* 202)

Sculpture and Painting
of the Heian Period

Sculpture and painting were also profoundly influenced by the
esoteric doctrines. Shingon favored an iconography of Tantrist divinities, who were connected with the five manifestations of the Bodhisattva Akasagarbha (Kokuzo in Japanese), personifying infinite wisdom, and an inexhaustible faculty for providing good fortune and
happiness. Depicted seated on a lotus stem, on the top of a rock that
symbolizes the sacred mountain Sumeru emerging from the sea, the
Bodhisattva is often rendered, in statuary, not as a single figure but in
a series of five images (Godai Kokuzo), whose different hand positions
allude to the projection of his powers in the five directions of space.
This figurative canon is represented here by the group of composed
and opulent statues of the Jingoji in Kyoto (Figure 54). They were
created in the middle of the ninth century and are an example of

THE GOLDEN AGE   101

57. Amida triad in gilded bronze. Flanking the figure of the Buddha Amitabha, and preceding him, as if in a celestial procession, are the Bodhisattvas Mahasthamaprapta (Seishi in Japanese) and Avalokitesvara (Kannon). A.D. 1148 (Heian Period). Sanzenin, Kyoto.

58. Detail of the profile of a wood statue of Amida Nyorai, the Buddha Amitabha. Twelfth century A.D. (Heian Period). Fukidera, Prefecture of Oita.

59. Rock relief of the Amida triad. The seated figure of the Buddha is flanked by the Bodhisattvas Seishi and Kannon in standing positions. The allegorical lotus flowers serve as throne and pedestals. Eleventh or twelfth century A.D. (Heian Period). Oyadera, Prefecture of Tochigi.

Following pages:

60. In the foreground, the stone head of a Buddha with traces of color. In the background are other Buddha and Bodhisattva figures. Rock sculpture. Eleventh or twelfth century A.D. (Heian Period). Prefecture of Oita.

complete and delicate stylistic unity. The highly refined inspiration of Indian esoteric iconography produces a certain sensuality in the treatment of the faces and bodies, which occurs often in the religious art of the epoch.

The iconographic repertory was dominated, however, by the Amidists. The cult of Amida, the Buddha of infinite virtues, was the leader of the Pure Land sects. Founded in China by Tao-ch'o (562–645), it was based on the authority of a first-century B.C. Sanskrit text, the *Sakhavativyuha*, which narrates that in the remote past the Bodhisattva Dharmakara pronounced forty-eight vows, one of which was to save all those who invoked his name. Later this Bodhisattva became the Buddha Amitabha, and, in accordance with his vows, he settled in the Pure Land of the Western Paradise, "a million billion Buddha Lands" away. This is the place of beatitude to which he brings all the creatures whose souls, according to the faith, are subject to birth and death. These ideas were introduced in Japan by monks such as Kuya (died 972) and Genshin (942–1017). Genshin's preaching, contained in a very popular tract, insisted on the horrors of hell and the delights of paradise, whose doors would magically open for anyone who invoked Buddha's name when about to die. The great success this idea of salvation obtained is attested to by the great number of paintings of "Amida's welcome," which were set next to the dying to give them comfort and help in their final hours. Already in China the sect had honored Amitabha by multiplying the number of his statues and paintings depicting the splendor of the Pure Land. In Japan also such iconography was exalted.

Buddhism finally found in the cult of Amida, stripped as it was of every speculative and conceptual element, the most convenient way of bringing a message of salvation to the masses. In 1124 Ryonin taught that the recitation — sometimes repeated up to sixty thousand times a day — of the formula *Namu Amida Butsu*, "all honor to the Buddha Amitabha," was the sure way of gaining the paradise of the Pure Land. Honen Shonin (1133–1212), who lived in a period of

grave material and spiritual crisis, went so far as to say that the great limitations of one's own forces must necessarily lead to faith in a greater force, that of the Buddha Amida; therefore one was not to stop repeating Amida's name with all one's heart: "Whether you walk or lie down, you must not interrupt this practice, not even for a second." Only in this way was it certain that the Buddha Amida would descend to the dying man, to cut the hair linking him with life and to take the liberated soul to the Pure Land paradise. A picture of this place of eternal beatitude is to be seen in the mural paintings of the Byodoin (Figure 55): its pavilions, verandas, a little bridge, a series of elect figures immersed in the serene atmosphere of a splendid empyrean are the projection of a human world in an other-worldly, divine sphere.

The subject is also treated by the sculpture of the period, a great number of whose works are dedicated to Amida. In the Byodoin there is the figure in gilded wood of the Amida Nyorai (Figure 56). The pure figure of the Buddha Amida, who looks at the faithful with understanding, reflects the sentimental tone of Heian period society. It is an artistic composition of infinite refinement that emerges from the splendor of the gold and the rich treatment of even minor elements — the inlay work of the double halo and the large nimbus, for instance. The tiny figures surrounding the Buddha represent spiritual beings and musicians with flowing garments, seated on symbolic lotus thrones (the lotus being the flower that grows immaculate in the mud, just as the elect remain uncontaminated by the baseness of the world). Sculptured by Jocho (died 1057), one of the greatest Japanese wood sculptors, the work is one of the principal images of Amidism. Another is the gilded bronze triad of the Kyoto Sanzenin (Figure 57) that, almost a century later, shows in the total fleshiness of the figures the prevalence of the tendency to humanize the divinities. The minor figures in front of the Buddha, which according to iconographic convention precede Amida's train, represent the Bodhisattvas Seishi and Kannon (in Sanskrit, Mahasthamaprapta, and Avalokitesvara). The latter holds the lotus flower on which he will take the souls of the dead to the Pure Land paradise.

Another image of Amida in the Fukidera temple in the prefecture of Oita (Figure 58 is a detail of the profile of this statue) is a superb example of the technique of sculpturing in soft wood, the leading technique of the time. Gilded or left in its natural color, wood from this time on is the material used for statues that for their immediacy of stylistic effect and fine execution have no equal in all Asia. Jocho is counted among the great perfecters of wood sculpture, since he replaced the technique of working on one block, which always presented problems of cracking with that of sculpturing the work in separate pieces, which were then fastened together.

Stone and especially rock sculpture (the latter cut directly from cliffs, etc.) was more limited, but came to represent a phenomenon directly connected with the mountain temples, documenting the meaning and purpose of religious devotion in the most celebrated pilgrimage spots. Figure 59 shows a triad of Amida, with the Bodhisattva figures standing on lotus flowers, sculptured in high relief on the rocky wall near the Oyadera, a temple in the prefecture of Tochigi. This work was executed in either the eleventh or twelfth century and is part of a group of reliefs with a votive function, according to a custom with which are connected certain contemporary rock sculptures from the prefecture of Oita. In the foreground of Figure 60 is the head of a Buddha that still bears traces of color on its face and headdress. In this example the refinement of the modeling quite outdoes the usual rigidity and uncertainty with which the Japanese sculptor, because of inexperience, usually treats the stone, as is shown by the much more rigid figures in the background.

Besides sculpture, the religious iconography of the Heian period was widely used in painting, where the same themes often took a more idiosyncratic development. Figure 62 illustrates, in a rare pictorial

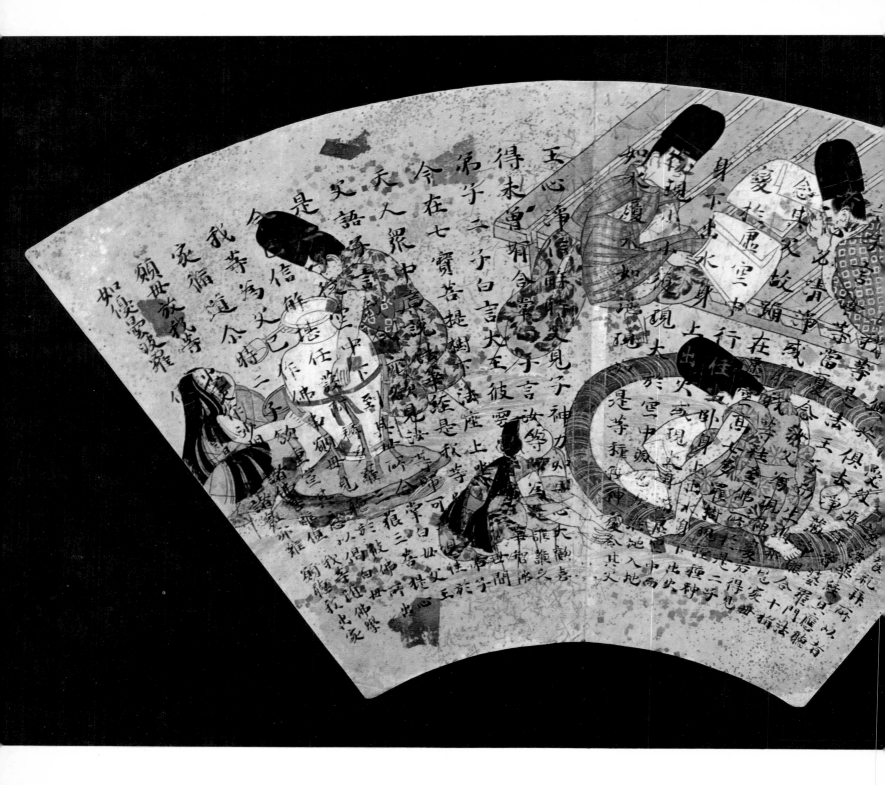

rendering, a Kokuzo Bosatsu (the Bodhisattva Akasagarbha). The severity of the style, so congenial to the figure's highly intellectual iconographic type, is not impaired by the miniaturist treatment of the work. The same can be said for the Fugen Bosatsu (Figure 63). Here too the attention given to detail, almost more graphic than pictorial, achieves a miniaturist effect yet verifies at the same time the definition of Heian period hieratic painting as "miniatures of great size."

In the last phase of this period the sacred paintings were flanked by other pictorial works executed either for religious celebration or for spiritual edification. These were illuminated manuscripts, executed on rolls or fan-shaped sheets, usually illustrating the *sutras* or containing passages from them. In the fan-shaped page from a volume that has the text of the *lotus sutra* (Figure 61), the scenes of artisans at work create a tone of private devotion, of the secular interpretation of a religious fact; they also mark the development of an art that has be-

61. A page of the so-called *sutra of the lotus on a fan* (Senmen Hokke-kyo Sasshi). Painted in color on paper, with calligraphy in black ink. Height, 10 inches; upper arch, 19.5 inches long. Second half of the twelfth century A.D. (Heian Period). (Tokyo National Museum).

62. Detail from a roll (*kakemono*) depicting the Bodhisattva Akasagarbha (Kokuzo Bosatsu); painted on silk: 4 feet 4 inches by 33 inches. Middle of the twelfth century A.D. (Heian Period). (Tokyo National Museum).

Following page:
63. Detail from *kakemono* depicting the Bodhisattva Samantabhadra (Fugen Bosatsu), symbol of universal wisdom. Painted on silk: 5 feet 3 inches by 29 inches. First half of the twelfth century A.D. (Heian Period). (Tokyo National Museum).

come conscious of the peculiarities of Japanese life and customs. This is the beginning of *yamato-e* (yamato painting), so-called to distinguish it from *kara-e* (Chinese painting); here also is one of the first characteristic syntheses of design and calligraphy that gives later Japanese painting an unmistakable and expressive originality.

Inherited from China along with its ideography, calligraphic art developed autonomously in Japan, gradually adapting the graphic signs to indigenous tastes, in an accentuated tendency toward cursive forms. Texts from the Heian period are generally in Chinese, which was still the official language, but Japanese was ever more frequently used in the attempt to make the national idiom an instrument of literary expression. The invention of a syllabic alphabet, *kana*, attributed to Kobo Daishi, aided this process, which had already been set in motion by the poets. The successful use of Japanese as a literary language was achieved, above all, by the women writers of the Heian court. The masterpiece of the literature of this period is a novel, the *Genji Monogatari* ("The Tale of the Genji") the story of the so-called Shining Prince, which was written around the year 1000 by an imperial lady-in-waiting, the noblewoman Murasaki Shikibu. Numerous other famous works of this period were written by women. The Heian civilization gave great prominence to women, at least above certain social levels; and the entire society was profoundly imbued with feminine elements. They gave to the period a mark of refined delicacy, and sometimes effete aestheticism, signs of the decadence that soon led to a revolutionary change in the government and culture of Japan.

THE GOLDEN AGE 107

THE MILITARISTIC MIDDLE AGES

The Kamakura Period

From the eleventh century on, Japan's golden civilization of peace and tranquility moved toward a fatal decline. The political power of the Fujiwara family was nearing its end. The Emperor Go-Sanjo (1034–1073) succeeded in reconquering the power of the state; but his son Shirakawa (1053–1129), a profoundly pious soul, could not resist the pressure of the clergy, and was so excessively generous with donations and privileges that he provoked terrible financial difficulty for the state treasury. One can get an idea of this by considering that in his reign, from 1072 to 1086, twenty-one temples were erected, not counting reliquaries and many other religious buildings; 5,470 religious paintings and about 35,000 statues of Buddha (127 of which were over sixteen feet high) were commissioned — all in only fourteen years. Perhaps it goes without saying that this religious exaltation — which among other things led the emperor to issue a law against hunting and fishing and required the liberation of all hawks and the destruction of all nets — threw the nation first into economic ruin and then into the arms of an incipient feudalism.

The great Tendai and Shingon monasteries became dangerous power centers. On the one hand, they had accumulated vast land holdings; on the other, they maintained seasoned armies of monks and mercenaries, which assaulted and burned neighboring monasteries, and, to force the government's hand, often made threatening incursions in Kyoto. The court aristocracy, especially the Fujiwara, thought they could protect themselves and salvage their positions by asking for help from the military nobility, which had consolidated itself in the provinces. For centuries, the families that had drifted away from the capital, in order to escape the pressure of the omnipotent Fujiwara, and the branches of the imperial family excluded from succession to the throne had built up vast landed estates there. Almost totally autonomous, they had few scruples about either defending this land and increasing it by force of arms. This worthy military aristocracy, when the opportune moment came, knew just how to establish itself once again in court life and strengthened its prestige amid the continual strife of the intrigue-ridden later Heian age.

The most powerful families were the Taira and the Minamoto, who shared vast property holdings in the southwestern and northeastern regions of the country. Through their active participation in the court struggles, they ended by confronting one another. Their power grew until, in 1155, taking advantage of a contested succession to the throne, the two houses entered into an open struggle, each one backing its own pretender. At the beginning of the bloody civil war, which was to last thirty years, the Taira took over the state power with Kiyomori (1118–1181); but at the end, after many ups and downs, the Minamoto overwhelmed the Taira in the naval battle of Dannoura (1185). During this last battle the Emperor Antoku was drowned, and with him the sword that had been one of the three sacred ensigns of Japanese sovereignty was lost. The loss of legitimacy was more than symbolic, however. The victor of Dannoura, the head of the Minamoto, Yoritomo (1148–1199) was given the title of Generalissimo (Shogun) and in 1192 set himself up as head of a military government that took the name of *bakufu*, that is, tent government. This event brought the Heian period to a dramatic end and marked the official beginning of the feudal epoch. The struggles of the Taira and the Minamoto form the basis of later Japanese epics, in which the rough warriors of

64. Todaiji: Detail of the main gateway to
the temple, the southern gate, or *nandaimon*. A.D. 1199 (Kamakura Period). Prefecture of Nara.

65. Kenchoji: The entrance portico of the temple. A.D. 1251 or 1253 (Kamakura Period). Prefecture of Nara.

66. Engakuji. *Shariden* (reliquary hall). Height: 34 feet 5 inches. A.D. 1279 or 1282 (Kamakura Period). Prefecture of Kanagawa.

the Minamoto from the Kanto region face the refined Taira, who are irremediably defeated by the customs and weaknesses of the court.

In the new capital of Kamakura, not far from present-day Tokyo, Yoritomo established a political and administrative system that, amid changes of fortune and precarious attempts to restore the empire, was to last until 1867. The powers of the state were transferred into the hands of the shogun and his own regents, while the emperors continued to live in the Kyoto court apparently undisturbed, keeping only their honorific attributes and undergoing the ever more weighty interference of the shogunate in court matters and the designation of their own heirs and regents. The new government at Kamakura functioned under a strong central administration, and the provinces were put under the control of functionaries whose duties were both military and fiscal. The shogunate headquarters boasted of nearly two thousand military houses who had sworn loyalty and had been called up as men of the house. On Yoritomo's death in 1199, a crisis arose over the succession, but the members of the Hojo family soon took over the government, keeping it until 1333 as regents, and greatly increasing the prestige of the Kamakura shogunate with an energetic and stable administration. The capital was transformed from a simple fishing village (which it was during Yoritomo's reign) to a relatively large city, where the Minamoto and the other families in power built their residences and where the new Buddhist sects lost no time in erecting their largest temples.

The social and philosophical conditions that developed as a result of the new political conditions of the Kamakura period caused renewed religious fervor. The civil wars had only served to emphasize and verify the Buddhist idea of the progressive degeneration of the world and the decadence of the law. Monastic life became more pervasively the ideal for those who wanted refuge from human society, which had shown such a willingness to shed blood. The monasteries were the sole refuge for arts and letters; the clergy was protected because it was by now the only class that furnished learned men, scribes, counselors, and

112 **JAPAN**

teachers for the warrior cults. Once the most humble *samurai* (warriors) and farmers were admitted into monasteries, however, the coating of nobility of the old religious orders was removed. The religious life that grew in influence was one that could count on a wide following for every message of hope it put forth. The resultant vulgarization of religious thought favored the translation of sacred texts into everyday language, and the secularized clergy that was formed married and had families in the conviction that they would thus be better able to understand the problems of the common people.

In the wake of Honen Shonin, who had founded the Pure Land sect (Jodo-shu), Shinran Shonin (1173–1262) set up the True Pure Land sect (Shin Jodo-shu), also called the True Sect (Shin-shu). This was a further simplification of the Buddha Amida cult, based on the principle that a single sincere invocation of the holy name was enough to save even a thoroughly bad man. At the same time the Lotus Sect (Hokke-shu), founded by Nichiren (1222–1282), began to spread. This assigned to Japan the historical function of saving Buddhism and reestablishing the original values of the faith transmitted by the sacred text, *the sutra of the lotus of good law. Namu Myoho Renge-kyo* — "all honor to the *sutra of the lotus*" — was the psalm which was to replace the superfluous and ineffective *Namu Amida Butsu* of the early Amida cults. Nichiren's message, which meant to preserve the historic mission of the nation, came at a time when Japan was passing through a terrible economic crisis and was under the threat of Chinese invasion. Two unsuccessful attempts at conquest were made in 1274 and 1281 by the Mongol, Kublai Khan (1224–1294), who, having made a conquest of almost all of Asia, had become the Chinese emperor. During both attempts at invasion, the wind of the Japan Sea had unleashed itself against the fleets of the invaders; it became known as the divine wind, *kamikaze*, and earned new merit for the Shinto and Buddhist religious orders, who had invoked it.

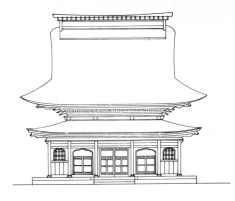

Elevation of the shariden, the reliquary hall of the Engakuji complex, a Zen temple in the Prefecture of Kanagawa, built between A.D. 1279 and 1282.

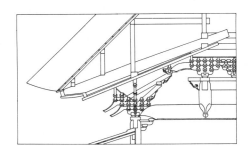

Beams and brackets of the Engakuji shariden.

Zen and Its Architecture

Contacts between Japan and China had been renewed in the first part of the Kamakura epoch. Many monks had gone to study in China, and Chinese monks had left their country to settle in the archipelago. These exchanges had favored the introduction of a new Buddhist sect, that of Ch'an (from Ch'an-na, meaning meditation or contemplation), which, with the Japanese name of Zen, was destined to exert a great influence on the spiritual life of the Japanese in the following centuries. Introduced into China in the sixth century A.D., according to tradition by the Indian patriarch Bodhidharma, this was a school of "Great Vehicle" Buddhism, which counseled the concentration and quieting of the human conscience as the interior action through which achievement of the spiritual values identified with the Buddha's nature could be realized.

Zen was transplanted to Japan at the end of the twelfth century by the monk Eisai (1141–1215) who, on his return from China in 1191, founded on the island of Kyushsu the first Zen monastery, the Shofukuji. Here the preaching of the new doctrine began. It immediately enjoyed the favor of the educated classes, particularly the military aristocracy. With its message of inner discipline and the untiring search for truth and illumination, Zen became the religious expression of the sober and austere concept of life that characterized *bushido* (the warrior's road), the severe code of morals and chivalry of the new military aristocracy, which was embodied in the so-called martial arts (*judo*, archery, sword-fighting, etc.) Through Zen, a realistic and virile concept of life predominated and the stamp of feminine refinement that had characterized the culture and art of the Heian period was completely effaced.

ON BUILDING A HOUSE

When building a house, it should be designed to suit the summer. In winter one can live anywhere, but in the hot weather an uncomfortable house is indeed trying.

There is no coolness in a deep pool, a shallow running stream is far cooler; and, in order to get a little light, a horizontal sliding door will open wider than a lifting shutter. But a high ceiling would make the winter seem colder and the lamp give but little light.

Before finishing, it is generally admitted that a spare room will add to one's comfort; it will be found useful for many purposes.
Kenko: *Tsure-zure Gusa*, translated by Porter
(*p*. 48)

67. Tenryuji: The garden with its small lake and rocks facing the temple A.D. 1345 (Nanboku-cho Period). Kyoto.

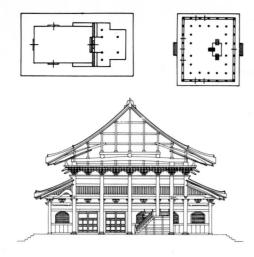

Plans and transverse section of a typical Zen temple meditation hall.

MEMORIES OF A HERMITAGE

Ceaselessly the river flows, and yet the water is never the same, while in the still pools the shifting foam gathers and is gone, never staying for a moment. Even so is man and his habitation.

In the stately ways of our shining Capital the dwellings of high and low raise their roofs in rivalry as in the beginning, but few indeed there are that have stood for many generations. This year falling into decay and the next built up again, how often does the mansion of one age turn into the cottages of the next. And so, too, are they who live in them. The streets of the city are thronged as of old, but of the many people we meet there how very few are those that we knew in our youth. Dead in the morning and born at night, so man goes on forever, unenduring as the foam on the water.

And this man that is born and dies, who knows whence he came and whither he goes? And who knows also why with so much labour he builds his house, or how such things can give him pleasure? Like the dew on the morning glory are man and his house, who knows which will survive the other? The dew may fall and the flower remain, but only to wither in the morning sun, or the dew may stay on the withered flower, but it will not see another evening.

Kamo No Chomei: *The Ten Foot Squre Hut* translated by Sadler (*pp.* 1–2)

68. Idealized portrait of the Indian Buddhist monk Asanga, known in Japan as Muchaku. The sculpture, of painted wood, is the work of Unkei and his school. Height of the entire statue: 6 feet 2 inches. A.D. 1208 (Kamakura Period). Kofukuji, Nara.

The constants of sobriety and austerity were naturally reflected also in the arts. In architecture the preference of the period was for simple and unadorned structures. The *buke-zukuri* (military style), became characteristic of residential construction. Surrounded by ditches and stockades, buildings were no longer set around a garden, but were collected into a single body under the same roof, or under a group of roofs set close together. Religious architecture, following the renewed contact with China, was modified according to two styles: the *tenjiku-yo*, the so-called Indian style, which was actually introduced from southern China, and the *kara-yo*, the Chinese style, so called to distinguish it from the *wayo* or national style. Many temples that had been built in the *tenjiku-yo* style were destroyed during the civil wars; among them was the Todaiji, which, together with the Kofukuji, had been one of the major propagation centers of Japanese Buddhism. The reconstruction work on the Todaiji, patronized by the court and the shogunate, was entrusted to Chogen, a monk who had studied the *tenjiku-yo* style in China and who was chosen head of a committee for the collection of the funds necessary for the work. In collaboration with the Chinese sculptor Chen Ho-ch'ing, who had come with him to Japan, Chogen saw to the planning and realization of the new buildings.

Today only the campanile and the great southern gate (*nandaimon*) still exist. The latter (Figure 64) epitomizes the characteristics of the new version of *tenjiku-yo* style, whose building technique makes use of large wooden beams set for the most part in rigidly straight lines. Vertical emphasis is entrusted to the increased number of rows of brackets, which often consist only of two wings set directly into the shaft of the columns, without the use of the intermediary capital. The roofs are frequently double, with a tile covering and a typical pavilion form. Some characteristics of the *tenjiku-yo* style seem to be the same as those of the *kara-yo* style: the bracketing, the tiles, and the roofs seem to carry on a Chinese architectural tradition without much change. But the *kara-yo* can be distinguished chiefly by its plans, utilized for monasteries, which restore the ancient rectangular layout, with the regular arrangement of the larger edifices along a central axis. The style was used in the Chinese Ch'an temples of the southern Sung dynasty (1127–1279), and was introduced in Japan by Eisai and used for the first time in 1202 for the construction of the Kenninji in Kyoto. The five great Zen monasteries of the Kamakura period were built in this style: the Kenchoji, Engakuji, Jufukuji, Jochiji, and Jomyoji. The Kenchoji is among the few surviving examples. Built in the middle of the thirteenth century, its access portal (Figure 65) has the long, square beams characteristic of the style, set into the columns in a solid and linear composition. The wood, left in its natural color, sometimes has sculptural decoration, as is the case with the portico in the *shariden*, (hall of relics), of the Engakuji (Figure 66), with the typical yoke arch of Chinese derivation.

This temple, built in the second half of the thirteenth century, is considered one of the purest examples of *kara-yo*. The *shariden* is, moreover, a new interpretation of the reliquaries, which until then had been symbolically represented by pagodas. From the Kamakura period on, pagodas gradually lost their importance, and where they do not disappear altogether, they remain outside the main enclosure, while inside there are the buildings more peculiar to Zen, such as the meditation hall (*zendo*) and, in particular, the gardens. One of these gardens, in the Tenryuji at Kyoto, was built in the first half of the fourteenth century, with a pool and rocks and some slabs that form a stone bridge; it is illustrated in Figure 67. The function of such gardens, which are common to both *kara-yo* and *tenjiku-yo* architectural styles, is essentially that of dissolving the architectural structure into the natural surroundings. To the natural element is left the task of coordinating the proportions and lines of the buildings, by employing patterns and forms that erase any pretension to monumental effect and mediate between the architectural work and the setting, between man and nature.

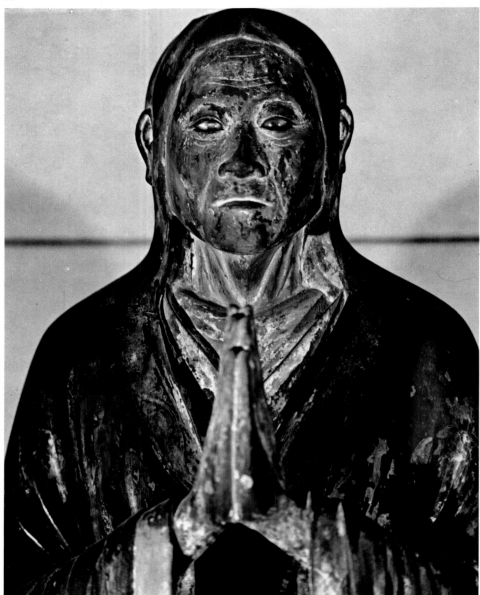

69. Anonymous portrait of Mawarajo. Wood sculpture. Twelfth century A.D. Sanjusangendo, Myohoin, Kyoto.

THE ACCOMPLISHMENTS OF A GENTLEMAN

Now as to a man's accomplishments, he must first of all be well read in books and familiar with the teachings of the sages. Next, though it be not his chief care, he should acquire a good handwriting; for it will assist him in his studies. Next he should apply himself to the art of medicine; for, if he be not a doctor, he can neither keep himself in good health, help others, nor even be faithful in his duties to his parents and lord. Next come archery and riding, which are included in the six accomplishments; he should certainly know something of them. In fact he must not be without literary and military skill and some knowledge of medicine; for, if he has these, he will not be called a man in vain. Then, as eating is natural to all, to be able to prepare a tasteful dish is a great advantage. And after that some technical ability (wood carving, etc.) is often of great service.

In all matters other than these, too great proficiency is a dishonour to a gentleman. As for the magical art of governing by the wonderful power of music and poetry, though both the Sovereign and his statesmen once thought highly of it, yet in these latter days it seems to be growing rare to rule a country thus. In the same way, though gold is very excellent, it cannot be compared with iron for utility.

Kenko: *Tsure-zure Gusa*, translated by Porter (*pp.* 94–95)

Zen in the Figurative Arts

As a form of thought that leads man back to his own inner dimension, molding his capacity for profound spiritual introspection, Zen also influenced the figurative arts to a great degree. Instead of the images of a composite pantheon, it preferred the depiction of the most significant moments of Zen teaching and illumination, and celebrated the figures of the patriarchs, monks, illustrious personages, and even laymen whom history, if not always religion, pointed out as brilliant examples of intelligence and humanity. Art, therefore, was not so much glorification as it was commemoration; this characteristic was particularly emphasized by the Zen artists themselves. Their conception of creative activity was neither professional nor amateur in any usual sense. Instead, they set themselves the task of establishing a spiritual contact between masters and disciples, monks and laymen, expressing the salient points of Zen by plastic, pictorial, or calligraphic means. This attitude determined the concentration on portraiture both in sculpture and in painting.

The sculptural portrait reached one of its most intensely expressive moments with the work of Unkei (1148–1223). A large part of the statuary of this epoch belongs to his school, which is linked in many ways with the classical iconographic tradition. The group of statues of prelates in the Kofukuji in Nara stands out by the incisiveness of its

70. **Portrait of the Buddhist monk Muso Soseki, in the pose of a master facing his disciples. Wood sculpture. Height, 31 inches. A.D. 1327 (Kamakura Period). Zuisenji, Prefecture of Kanagawa.**

style. One of these (Figure 68) is the idealized, almost life-size portrait of the Indian monk Asanga, known in Japan as Muchaku, founder of the Hosso sect, which was brought to Japan during the first period of Buddhist preaching. In the proportions of the body, made heavy by the cloak, the statue reveals the ever-present influence of Chinese portraiture; but the crude and vigorous treatment of the face, the intense and concentrated expression, the purity of a lively inner spirituality, makes this one of the absolute masterpieces of Far Eastern portrait statuary. The portrait statue of Mawarajo, in the Myohoin at Kyoto (Figure 69), is of almost Alexandrian taste; the wrinkles of old age detract not at all from the vitality of the face. The limpid, penetrating eyes conceal, in the fixity of the glance, intense inner suffering and labor. The portrait of Muso Soseki in the Zuisenji (Figure 70) is more conventional; it shows the prelate seated in the usual pose of the master facing his disciples.

As a whole these sculptured portraits also reveal the prevalence of a realistic and virile conception of life, which very shortly became evident as well in works of more traditional iconographic sculpture. However, the iconography expresses itself in a great variety of forms and techniques. The rock reliefs in the prefecture of Oita (Figure 71) repeat with few variants an act of secular devotion. The graphic style of the princely image of the Buddha Maitreya, found in Onodera (prefecture of Nara) in a niche cut out of the rock wall, (Figure 72) is more original. Another highly typical and representative piece from the monumental

71. Rock reliefs of Buddhist subjects. Twelfth or thirteenth century A.D. (Heian-Kamakura periods). Prefecture of Oita.

sculpture of the epoch is the colossal image of Daibutsu, the Great Buddha, in the Kotokuin (Figure 73). This bronze statue is over thirty-six feet high. A strong chromatic effect is seen in the gilded effigies of the Senju Kannon (Kannon of the thousand arms) in the Myohoin (Figure 74), whose multiplicity of aspects, realized through repeated images, becomes the tangible symbol of the merciful compassion of the Bodhisattva who, because of his infinite capacity for love, Far Eastern iconography depicts with almost feminine features.

The contribution the Kamakura age made to religious iconography was in part due to the effort made by the nation to reconstruct the large monuments that had been destroyed or damaged during the civil wars. Great sculptors such as Kokei and his son Unkei, exponents of the school of Buddhist sculpture founded by Jocho in the Heian period, helped to restore some Buddhist monasteries in Nara, in particular the Kofukuji and the Todaiji. Their long and patient work, which lasted from 1180 to 1212, allowed Unkei to go deeply into a study of eighth-century Buddhist sculpture, and there is unmistakable influence in his work of its stylistic heritage. The Kongo Rikishi of the Todaiji, one of which is illustrated in Figure 75, derive directly from the iconographic types of the Shitsu Kongoshin and of the other Tenno (the kings of the sky), which represent the guardians of the four cardinal points, entrusted with the task of defending the world from the enemies of the law. The conception that inspired them created a specific iconographic category of Buddhist art, characterized by a crude and ruthless countenance symbolizing the rigor with which these guardians do their duty.

The Kongo Rikishi (Figure 75) is one of the two colossal sculptures set at the southern entranceway of the Todaiji. Unkei executed them in collaboration with Kaikei and twenty other artists, in 1203. Sculptured in separate blocks, which were later united, both statues are over twenty-six feet high. They are the largest existing wooden sculptures in the world. The powerful and raging manner of the figures, the impressive muscularity of their limbs, the flashing faces express, in all their force the holy anger that animates these valiant defenders of the faith. The exaggerated aspects of their anatomy, the excessively strong and indomitable expressions, in short the preference for an image that surpasses human limits, often makes this statuary seem mere caricature or grotesquerie. This is the case with the inaccessible and violent Konpira-o in the Myohoin (Figure 76), and the demoniacal, faunlike Tentoki in the Kofukuji (Figure 77). In the statue of Ashura-o in the Myohoin (Figure 78), whose four faces symbolize the omnipotence and all-embracing vision of this demon, the total expression is somewhat more composed. For all their excesses of exterior forms and expression, however, these works of art are compositions with a strong inner power.

The aesthetics peculiar to Zen exerted a vast influence in painting and calligraphy as well. Sun dynasty (960–1279) Chinese art had formed the largest synthesis of Buddhist Confucian and Taoist ideals; this artistic synthesis in its turn contributed to the philosophic definition of the Chinese doctrine of Ch'an. The black-and-white China-ink drawings of nature (in Japanese, *suiboku* or *sumi-e*) remain the most characteristically Zen artistic accomplishments. They express at the same time the secular and religious ideal of the wise man in communion with nature that had been postulated long before by Taoism and only later by Ch'an. The humble dwelling among the mountains, the pavilion that rises on the banks of a lake, express a concept of life that unfolded and spread over every aspect of culture both material and spiritual, until it became a fact of custom and fashion.

National Styles in Painting and Literature

Yamato-e or painting in the Japanese national style, which originated in the preceding Heian period, illustrates, on rolls that unfold hori-

zontally, the history of the temples and the biographies of illustrious religious personalities of the time. Figure 79 shows a scene from the *Ippen Shonin Eden*, which describes the life and holy works of the monk Ippen (1239–1289), who was one of the propagators of the Amida faith in Japan. This painting shows an animated scene of country life and exemplifies the increasingly evident tendency in Japanese painting to approach reality in a purely documentary or narrative vein. The same tendency is seen in the illustrations of historic works, such as the rolls of the *Heiji Monogatari* ("History of the Heiji Era"), (Figure 80), which recreate bloody episodes of war, tumults, intrigues, and civil rebellions. The narrative, the historiographic aim, and the need to render reality as faithfully as possible, lead to the crudeness of the paintings' execution.

The same orientation is to be seen in literature, especially in the historical novels of the time. The *Heike Monogatari* ("History of the

73. The Daibutsu (Great Buddha). Colossal bronze statue in the Kotokuin, in the Prefecture of Kanagawa. Height: 37 feet 3 inches. Circa A.D. 1252.

74. Senju Kannon (Kannon of the thousand arms). Gilded wood sculpture. Height of the figures: 5 feet 7 inches. Twelfth or thirteenth century A.D. (Heian-Kamakura periods). Sanjusangendo, Myohoin, Kyoto.

Heike or Taira"), a twelfth- or early thirteenth-century work, drew its inspiration from the recent struggles between the great fuedal families. The protagonists are no longer the cold and conventional court personages of the works of the Heian period, but instead impetuous warriors. The descriptions of battle and death take the place of the obsolete love battles and give a tragic tone to the pages of an epic that renders more the pain than the heroism of the civil war. The writers of the Heian period, immersed in a superficial atmosphere of joyful or tender thoughtlessness, rarely evoke the past except in a tone of sweetness; with the disappearance of their world, the nostalgia and regret for that past predominate and become the dominant theme of the new literature. *Hojoki* ("Memories of the Ten Foot Square Hut") by Kamo no Chomei (1154–1216) and *Tsurezure-gusa* ("Variety of Moments of Idleness") by Kenko Hoshi (1283–1350) can in certain respects be compared to *Makura no Soshi* ("The Notes of the Pillow") by Sei

75. Kongo Rikishi (the lightning bearer), protective divinity of Buddhism. Wood sculpture by Unkei and Kaikei. Height: 27 feet 4 inches. A.D. 1203 (Kamakura Period). Nandaimon, Todaiji, Nara.

76. Konpira-ǫ, the implacable guardian of the Buddhist faith. Thirteenth century A.D. (Kamakura Period). Sanjusangendo, Myohoin, Kyoto.

77. Tentoki. Detail from a pair of monstrous spirits, sculptured in the form of lantern-holders. Height, 29.3 inches. Painted wood. A.D. 1215 (Kamakura Period). Kofukuji, Nara.

Following pages:
78. Ashura-o, a demon of Indian mythology included in the Buddhist pantheon as a protective divinity. Its many heads express its infinite prophetic qualities. Thirteenth century A.D. (Kamakura Period). Sanju-sangendo, Myohoin, Kyoto.

Shonagon, a woman writer of the Heian period; but the tone is much more bitter and shows the effects of a characteristically Buddhist pessimism. Both works gather together meditations and thoughts that their writers have allowed to mature in their hermitage, after having taken up a monastic life in the knowledge of the utter vanity and mortality of earthly values.

In the literature of the time the uncertain political conditions are painfully alive and the suffering is clear. Some voices were raised in defense of the ancient traditional institutions that have collapsed, but even in such works, one has the feeling that the Japanese nation is about to precipitate into fatal disorder. Chikafusa Kitabatake (1293–1354), in a work on the legitimacy of the imperial power, *Jinno Shotoki* ("Memories of the Legitimate Succession of the Divine Emperors"), pleads for the obedience of the subjects to the emperor, who is god-king. Other works extol the courage and loyalty of the warrior, describing a world of honor whose emblems are the sword and cherry blossom; the sword is a personification of the soul of the *samurai*, the cherry blossom the symbol of the fragility of his existence. Just as the petals of the early spring flower fall with the first breath of wind, so the *samurai* does not hesitate to give his life valiantly for his lord, or sacrifice it honorably by means of the slowest and most horrifying death of all, the cutting of one's abdomen.

By the same principles of honor, the nobility was divided into two camps. One faction sided with the shogun, the other with the emperor. The situation afforded little prospect for peaceful agreement. In 1333 the Emperor Go-Daigo (1288–1339) made an attempt to restore the imperial power and in fact succeeded in defeating the Kamakura shogunate. But the restoration was short-lived, because the irremediable conflict between the court nobility and the military aristocracy (the latter having lost prestige because of the newly powerful imperial throne) sparked new struggles that wasted the entire country. Massacre and disorder were the rule. Between 1336 and 1392 occurred the great dynastic schism that historians call the Nanboku-cho period, the period of the southern and northern courts. Two dynasties contended for the throne: a northern dynasty at Kyoto, and a southern one in the mountains of Yoshino, south of Nara. During the long struggle, which terminated with the restitution of the Kyoto dynasty, Japan was lacerated by anarchy and devastation. Eventually a branch of the Minamoto family, the Ashikaga, got the upper hand and reestablished the shogunal government, moving its seat to the Muromachi quarter of Kyoto, where the palace of the family was.

The Muromachi Period

The restoration of Kyoto as full-fledged capital gave a new look to the shogunate. Although the military authorities had seized the imperial capital, they ended by absorbing the manners of the old court nobility. Like them they built palaces, protected temples, respected and cultivated a refined upbringing, and surrounded themselves with pomp emulating that of the imperial court. A typical figure of the period remains the third shogun, Ashikaga Yoshimitsu (1358–1408). In him warlike gifts were perfectly fused with an elevated and aristocratic spirit. Having been given the title King of Japan by the Chinese emperor, at a time when the imperatives of commerce rendered even an act of subjection to China acceptable, he treated the reigning Japanese emperor virtually as an equal, had his wife named empress mother, and celebrated his son's coming-of-age with a sumptuous ceremony worthy of a royal prince.

The bringing together of the two courts, although realized in a climate of outward magnificence, had little positive effect on the nation's stability or well-being. The unremitting interference of the shogunate with the court, together with the tight controls it lay on its revenue, led the imperial institution into an indigence aggravated even

further by the loss of the income from its provincial fiefs, which had become the property of the military nobility. On the death of the Emperor Go-Tsuchimikado (1442–1500), the august body was allowed to lie in front of the imperial palace for forty days, because of a lack of funds for the funeral. A feudal lord, Sasaki Takayori, finally put up the money for the ceremony. Another emperor, Go-Nara (1497–1557), was obliged to make a living by selling his autographs. The crisis was felt throughout the entire nation. Under the eighth shogun, Ashikaga Yoshimasa (1436–1490), the coffers of the treasury were emptied to pay the expenses of a costly life of luxuries and patronage, while the population was decimated by hunger, famine, and the plague. The request of a loan from China was preceded domestically by the imposition of still more burdensome taxes.

Economic collapse and progressive weakening of the shogunate's policies hastened the rise of the provincial nobility, above all the great feudal lords who had set up military regimes in their own territories, hiring troops and employing *samurai* as warrior-vassals. The increased power of the feudal lords (*daimyo*) threw the Ashikaga government into a crisis, since the *daimyo* could evade paying the prescribed tribute, while at the same time extending their own territories at the expense of their weaker neighbors. The government officials assigned to control the provinces themselves became military chieftains and feudatories,

79. Scene from a roll (*makimono*) illustrating the biography of the monk Ippen (Ippen Shonin Eden), painted by Hogen En-i. A.D. 1299 (Kamakura Period). Colored paint on paper: 15 inches by 26 feet 4 inches. (Tokyo National Museum).

claiming their posts as hereditary. All of this, combined with the
struggles among the feudatories themselves for the highest posts, soon
threw the country into anarchy. The civil wars that broke out in
Onin days (the time of disorders) (1467–1468), devastated Kyoto and
marked the beginning of the period known as *sengoku-jidai* (the nation
of war). During this period Japan was reduced to a state of permanent
domestic struggle that starved the rural populations and prompted the
exodus from the land of its most valuable men, who either went into
the service of the local lords or gave themselves over to piracy.

Meanwhile, the need for military supplies and the increase in exchanges with the Asian continent fostered industries and trade. These
became the perquisites both of the feudal lords and of the monasteries,
which turned their attention to them as new sources of profit. Even the
resumption of trade relations with China, which had been cut off by
the abortive Mongolian invasions during the thirteenth century, was
due to the initiative of the Buddhist clergy. The monk Muso Soseki
(1275–1351), who under the patronage of the Ashikagas had done his
utmost for the building of the Tenryuji, a temple dedicated to the
memory of the Emperor Go-Daigo, had proposed to Ashikaga Takauji
that the necessary funds be raised by sending two shiploads of salable
goods to China. In 1342, the first Tenryuji ships set sail. Soon followed
by others, they opened the way to a flourishing trade with China. But
the raids carried out along the Chinese coasts by Japanese pirates,
whose booty was divided with many feudatories along the coasts of the
archipelago, caused a setback in the negotiations aimed at establishing
regular exchanges between the two countries. An accord was reached
only in 1401. It was based on a system of credit sales, calling for an
official exchange of merchandise once every ten years. Later on the
accord was liberalized, to the point that in 1454 no less than ten ships
set sail in only one year: three represented the Tenryuji, for the
Ashikaga; two belonged to the Ise sanctuary, for the imperial family;
one was for the temple of Tonomine; one for the governor-general of
Kyushu; and the others for illustrious feudal families. The export
goods consisted of copper, sulfur, swords, and other objets d'art and
handicrafts, including fans and painted screens. The imports consisted
primarily of coins, medicines, books, silk, porcelain, and painted scrolls.

The contacts with the continent brought about by this traffic had
the effect of reinserting Japanese culture into the groove of Chinese
culture. Japan was soon penetrated by the influence of the arts of
China's Yuan (1279–1368) and Ming (1368–1644) dynasties, whose
decided tendency toward decoration then became the dominant
character in every facet of the artistic production of the time. Zen
ideals of simplicity of life and customs continued to be the basis of a
good deal of Japan's indigenous philosophical and religious thinking,
but at the pinnacle of culture and society a taste for the sumptuous
prevailed. A profusion of gold and colors adorned the interiors of
residences; furnishings became more elaborate and ostentatious.
Murals, screens, roll paintings, gold lacquers, and precious ceramics
abounded. Residential architecture gave growing importance to the
use of sculptural ornamentation and to gardens as an element mediating
between architectural structures and the natural environment.

Despite all the wealth and sumptuousness, the finest works of the
period still possess a linear elegance. A celebrated example of this is the
Kinkakuji or golden pavilion (Figure 81). Built by Yoshimitsu in 1397
at Kitayama, on the northern hills near Kyoto, the pavilion was part
of a large villa composed of thirteen buildings built around a garden
with a lake. After Yoshimitsu's death, the villa was converted into a
Buddhist temple, the Rokuonji, and the Kinkakuji was turned into a
hall of relics. The entire project was hybrid in style between the *shinden*
of the Heian period and the *buke-zukuri*. The Kinkakuji, the only
building of the group that survived (it was entirely rebuilt after a fire
in 1950, however), is made up of three stories surrounded with wide
verandas. Lacquer and gold-leaf decoration adorns both the outside
and inside of the building, in a marked contrast to the slim simplicity

of the structure. The broad roof covering of the second floor and the
upper roof, culminating in a phoenix, are austerely faced with bark.
Another example of this highly refined compositive architecture is the
Ginkakuji, or silver pavilion, built for a sophisticated coterie of artists
and monks by the shogun Yoshimasa (1434–1490) at Higashiyama,
on the eastern hills of Kyoto.

Noh, Zen and Other
Cultural Phenomena

Such coteries were more than simple gatherings of educated men;
they represented a characteristic aspect of the cultural life of the time.

80. Scene of the transfer of the imperial
court to Rokuhara. Detail from the roll
illustrating the history of the Heiji era
(*Heiji Monogatari Ekotoba*). Colored paint
on paper: 16.8 inches by 31 feet 5 inches.
(Tokyo National Museum).

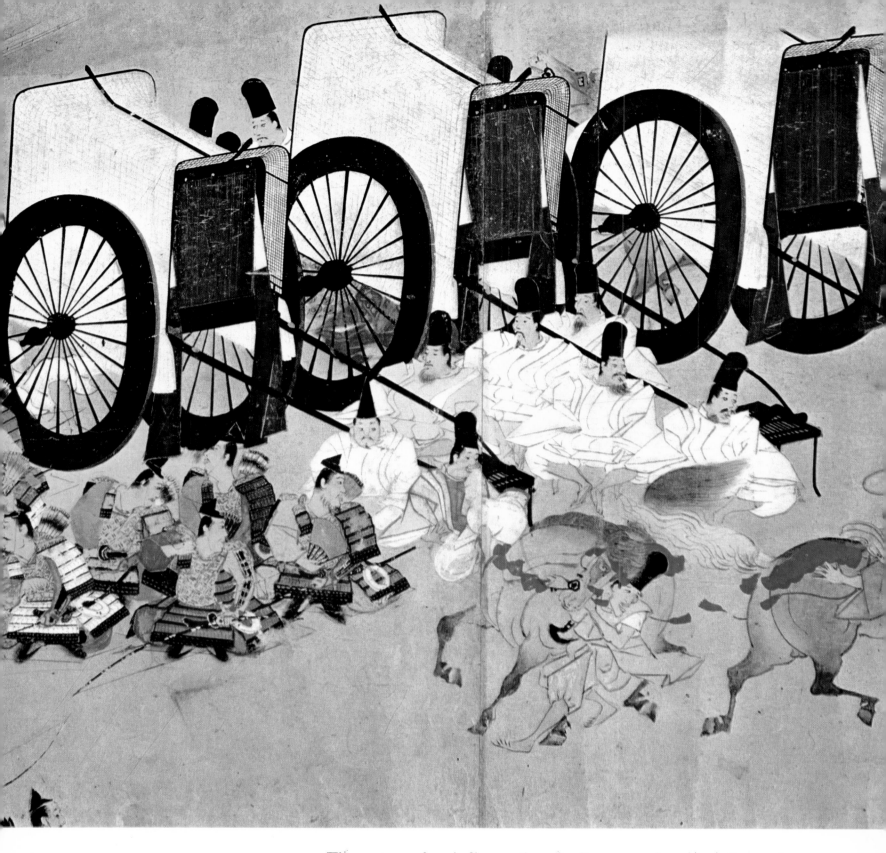

Following pages:
81. The Golden Pavilion (Kinkakuji). A.D. 1397 (Muromachi Period). It was rebuilt after a disastrous fire in 1950. The fire inspired Yukio Mishima's novel *Kinkakuji* Rokuonji enclosure, Kitaku, Kyoto.

The custom of periodic meetings for literary and poetical disputations had been introduced into the court centuries earlier. As patronage gained ground, the nobility began surrounding themselves with people who did not belong, properly speaking, to the world of the court, such as religious men and professional artists. In the Ashikaga epoch, thanks to the patronage accorded by Yoshimitsu to Kanami and Seami, the lyrical *noh* drama came into being. Having obtained economic security, the two artists had the leisure necessary to transform the old plays of popular theater into a highly noble and poetic dramaturgy. The birth of the *noh* can be seen as an exemplification of the new spiritual climate. A number of components were combined in the *noh* dramas, including folklore, the classical court literature, Shinto, and Buddhism. It is not going too far to say that the *noh* theater actually originated in the coterie of the Ashikaga, because it was precisely with the Ashikaga that a beginning was made in what today would be termed a cultural dialogue, where art, religion, and culture interact.

The meetings fostered an exchange of ideas unusual in an otherwise rigid society, in which men were enabled to see beyond their own concerns. Traditional poetry tournaments, fundamentally competitive, were transmuted into meetings for the composition of chain poetry, during which each participant collaborated in the work at hand with a certain number of verses. These were not only to provide an arena for competition or the display of genius or exceptional ability, however; the idea was rather that each should make his own contribution. This atmosphere at the meetings was often enhanced by the tea ceremony, which offered the pleasure of sipping a hot drink prepared in accordance with an aesthetic, almost a religious, ceremony, in an appropriate place, where at the same time one could enjoy pleasant conversation and the sight of artistic objects. These consisted of a painting, or a floral composition (*ikebana*), or even the tea sets themselves, of ceramics or lacquered crockery, simple yet refined, which were often the creations of the tea masters.

The tea ceremony, which had been introduced into Japan from China by the Zen masters, inspired the construction of special buildings: the tea pavilion and the tea house. The unadorned simplicity and modest dimensions of these architectural structures, which permitted them to be placed harmoniously into a landscape, symbolized somewhat the condition necessary for an individual to achieve, through the meditative *chado* (the tea road), a spiritual unity between the outer world and the inner world, considered indispensable for all acts of artistic and literary creation. Among the best exemplars in the *chado* style is the Togudo of the Jishoji in Kyoto (Figure 84), built in 1486 as the private chapel or study of Ashikaga Yoshimasa. Despite the continental Asian origin of the building type, the structure has an appearance that is typically Japanese, even to the vegetation covering its roof, which calls to mind the ancient insular architectural tradition. The building consists of a hall called the *dojunsai*, the first ancient example of a reading room, with a study alcove (*shoin*) built out from it onto a wood veranda.

Deriving from the architecture of the Zen monasteries, the tea house was one of the chief innovations in the residential architecture of the time. The new architecture was generally characterized by the use of woods that are left in their natural state and by constructions with square pillars and light ceiling woodwork. The floors of the rooms were covered with mats (*tatami*); the interior rooms were divided by sliding doors and screens. Wall shelves and niches were built into the main rooms, which were rendered more luminous by the windows of the *shoin*. This was a new departure in architecture, which found its definitive formulation in the *shoin* style of residential architecture. In it, the diagrammatic balance and symmetry of buildings, which had been the characteristic of the *shinden-zukuri*, gave way to structures in which the architecture aimed at fusion with nature. And this explains the continuing importance of the garden.

Zen symbolism had already brought into fashion the so-called closed landscape, which concentrated in a small space the various elements to be found in nature. The style had been used primarily in conjunction with the architectural structures of the *kara-yo* style and had been perfected by Muso Soseki in planning projects like the Saihoji and Tenryuji. Then, under the influence of landscape painting, artists like Sesshu (1420–1506) and Soami (d. 1525) carried out projects in which the classical elements of the *shinden* garden — lake, islands, tiny bridges — were no longer distributed in such a way as to create a rigid picture. Their topography, together with that of the architectural elements, now sought an effect that varied, depending on the vantage point from which the garden was viewed. Pavilions scattered along the banks of small lakes were *de rigeur*, and they became an integral part of the *shoin* gardens. From Zen, however, these gardens inherited the typical symbolism, which they developed to such an extent as to substitute,

82. Part of the dry garden of the Ryoanji complex. The gravel is thought to symbolize the sea, with rocks emerging from it, although other interpretations of the meaning of the garden have been made. Circa A.D. 1473 (Muromachi Period). Ukyoku, Kyoto.

83. "Winter landscape," painted by Sesshu Toyo in the second half of the fifteenth century A.D. (Muromachi Period). Ink on paper roll; 11.5 inches by 18.2 inches. (Tokyo National Museum).

Following page:
84. Jishoji. The Togudo pavilion, facing the lake. A.D. 1486 (Muromachi Period). Sakyoku, Kyoto.

for example, sand for water, creating the so-called dry garden: an area of ground, usually rectangular, covered with white sand or gravel, with a number of rocks emerging, as if from water. An example of this is the garden of the Ryoanji of Kyoto, one corner of which is illustrated in Figure 82. A rectangular surface, measuring 258 square yards, spreads out in front of the temple. Bordered by a rustic wall of clay, it is covered with gravel and studded with fifteen rocks. With the exception of the moss on the rocks, there is no vegetation. The gravel is raked up into small waves, and the rocks arranged in five groups, which are said to represent tigers crossing a river with their cubs. Known also as "the valley of the tigers returning to their lairs with their little ones," the garden was apparently inspired by a Chinese legend about a sovereign who, by his example of meekness and goodness, had succeeded in taming wild animals. In other gardens, a succession of stone slabs symbolizes a fording point or a pathway, alluding in certain cases to the road leading to illumination.

The painting of the Muromachi period also continued to draw inspiration from the Zen masters, and the artists of the Kano school excelled in the severe techniques of white and black, while the trend toward decoration was represented by the Tosa school. Sesshu Toyo remains the most eminent personality of the period, the unequaled master of mountain landscapes, executed with sharp strokes in a style full of a quite modern sensitivity. An example of this is his "Winter Landscape" (Figure 83) in China-ink and light colors on paper, a vigorous, personal interpretation of wild, inhospitable nature, in which man creates a secluded refuge with his architecture.

THE MILITARISTIC MIDDLE AGES 137

THE GROWTH OF THE CITIES

Japan and the West

The precariousness of the political situation during the Muromachi period did not hinder the renewed flourishing of culture and the arts. Under the impetus brought to the city and its cultural circles by the Ashikagas, Kyoto had grown into an important educational center, and libraries and schools had also been established at the various feudal seats. The Buddhist temples with their educational institutions had begun to impart the rudiments of knowledge to the inhabitants of even the most remote villages. Schools of art and industries had risen at the various fiefs and temples, and art and trade associations had been formed. Buddhist temples and Shinto sanctuaries had begun handling commercial traffic and had developed new urban concentrations. Up to the Kamakura period, Japan's only cities had been the great capitals. The other provincial centers, however important for the national economy, had remained ports or trade centers. Foreign trade, consolidating the economic power of merchants and shipowners, had paved the way for the formation of large settlements. The city of Sakai had even enjoyed a certain political independence, as a reward for the profits it assured the shogunate government. Maritime traffic became increasingly intense. By the middle of the sixteenth century, Japanese merchants were competing directly with the newly arrived Europeans in the ports of China; indeed, the Europeans had been putting in at the Japanese archipelago as well.

The earliest reports on Japan had come to Europe through Marco Polo (1254–1324), who had told stories of the immense wealth of Chipangu. The Spanish navigators had soon begun to follow the western routes in search of the countries described in *Il Milione* ("The Travels of Marco Polo"); the Portuguese had attempted to reach the "road of spices" by southern and eastern routes. The Cape of Good Hope, discovered in 1486 by Bartolomeo Diaz and rounded by Vasco da Gama in 1497, had opened the maritime gates to Asia. Alfonso d'Albuquerque took possession of Goa in 1510 and of Malacca in 1511. In 1522 the Portuguese settled at Ningpo, in 1544 at Amoy, and in 1577, they set up a trade base at Macao. In the same period they also visited Japan.

In 1542 or 1543, three Portuguese navigators, including Fernando Mendez Pinto, had by chance landed at Tanegashima, a small island south of Kyushu. They were on a Chinese junk headed for Macao, but were blown by a typhoon onto the Japanese coasts. Given a friendly welcome by the islanders, the three navigators lost no time in astonishing them with their weapons and instruments, which revealed the hitherto unsuspected technical and industrial superiority of Europe. The feudal lord of the island, Tanegashima Tokitaka (1528–1579), passing from his initial amazement to an objective assessment of the efficiency and firing range of the arquebuses, had the navigators teach him how they were used and how they were made, and placed an order for a supply of them with his weapons-makers. This gave rise to the *tanegashima*, which was not only the first Japanese firearm but evidently the first tangible result of the meeting between Japan and the West. Under its influence, the native arts of war evolved rapidly; hand-to-hand fighting gave way to mass combat. Methods of strategy

HAIKU

Summer grasses —
All that remains
Of soldiers' visions.

The winds of autumn
Blow: yet still green
The chestnut husks.

A flash of lightning:
Into the gloom
Goes the heron's cry.
                    Matsuo Basho (1644–1694)

Beautiful, seen through holes
Made in a paper screen:
The Milky Way.

Red sky in the morning:
Does it gladden you,
O snail?
                    Kobayashi Issa (1763–1828)
Bownas and Thwaite: *Japanese Verse* (*pp.* 112–13, 123)

85. View of the Matsumoto castle in winter. A.D. 1594–1597 (Momoyama Period). Matsumoto, Prefecture of Nagano. The art of castle-building in Japan, between the end of the sixteenth and the beginning of the seventeenth centuries, is marked by the convergence of traditional fortified architecture of Japan with European building techniques.

and defense had to be changed. And all this occurred in a period of intensified domestic struggles.

The insurrections of the great feudal lords against the government of the Ashikagas plagued the nation for a number of decades, up to the time that order was gradually restored by three great military leaders: Oda Nobunaga, Toyotomo Hideyoshi, and Tokugawa Ieyasu. The period is known as that of the military dictatorships. Oda Nobunaga (1534–1582) overthrew the shogunate of the Ashikagas in 1573, bringing half of Japan under his sway, and in 1576 took up residence in the castle of Azuchi, from which he directed the political life of the nation. Toyotomi Hideyoshi (1535–1598) succeeded to Nobunaga in 1582 and transferred the government to Momoyama, near Kyoto, where in 1594 he had the castle of Fushimi built. His dream of a universal empire extending from Korea to China resulted in a period of war expeditions overseas. These were not successful, but by concentrating the energies of the Japanese outside the archipelago, they brought domestic peace. At the death of Hideyoshi, the governing power was taken over by Tokugawa Ieyasu (1542–1616) who, in the battle of Sekigahara, destroyed the power of the remaining hostile coalitions.

The Tokugawa

In 1603 Ieyasu was given the title of shogun and set up a new military government at Edo (the Tokyo of today), in the eastern part of the country, the same region where Kamakura was located. From the new capital Ieyasu reorganized the political life of the nation and imposed a form of absolute government which curbed the power of the feudal lords. In order to insure their unconditional allegiance to him, he subjected these feudal lords to the direct control of a state council and divided them into three different categories. The first two were made up of feudatories tied to Tokugawa by bonds of kinship and long friendship respectively; the third cateogry comprised those who had subjected themselves to Tokugawa only after the battle of Sekigahara, and whom Ieyasu had generously spared. Needless to say it was on the latter that suspicion constantly fell; as a result, their fiefs were distributed in a strategic manner so that they always remained under the control of the more trusted feudatories. Some time later an indiscrimate excess of caution dictated a law whereby all feudatories had to spend a period in the service of the shogun. This law, called service rotation, obligated the feudatories to reside in Edo for a certain time; during the period when they could return to their fiefs, they had to leave their families in the capital, for all intents and purposes as hostages. Their faithfulness was thus assured.

But this was not all: the periodic shifting from one place to the other and the need to keep up a second residence in the capital, with all the expenses of maintenance and representation that this entailed, made such inroads on the feudal lords' incomes that it prevented them from becoming more powerful economically and therefore politically. The example of the unfortunate fate of the Ashikagas, moreover, induced the new regime to forbid the feudatories to set up personal relationships with the court aristocracy. The military nobility were even forbidden to enter Kyoto, the imperial capital. Other limitations were contemplated in a series of regulations, for both the court nobility and the military nobility, which Ieyasu laid down in 1615. Observance of the ordinance of the shogun was assured at Kyoto by the presence of a government commissioner. The emperor, as the people's representative with the divinities, was restrained from meddling in politics or the affairs of the government, and was required rather to dedicate himself in all tranquility to study and the arts. Princes of royal blood were obliged to embrace religious life, with the sole exception of the heir to the throne, who was allowed to marry, but who had to choose

86. View of the massive wall and the beams of the buildings of Kumamoto castle. A.D. 1607 (Edo, or Tokugawa, Period). Chausuyama, Kumamoto.

Following pages:
87. View of the stone, wood, and masonry of the Kumamoto castle. The leaning, sloping tile roofs form ample gables on the facades. A.D. 1607 (Edo, or Tokugawa, Period). Chausuyama, Kumamoto.

Elevation of Tsuyama castle, eighteenth century A.D. (Edo Period). Prefecture of Okayama.

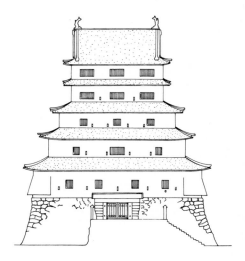

88. Detail from the Kumamoto castle: the facade of a castle building. A.D. 1607 (Edo Period). Chausuyama, Kumamoto.

THE INTRODUCTION OF FIREARMS

To the south of Osumi [Province] 18 *ri* off the shore, there is an island called Tanegashima. . . . During the Temmon Era [1532–1554], on the 25th of the eighth month of the year of the Water and the Hare [1543], there appeared off our western shore a big ship. No one knew whence it had come. It carried a crew of over a hundred whose physical features differed from ours, and whose language was unintelligible, causing all who saw them to regard them suspiciously. Among them was a Chinese scholar of whose family or given name no one was certain, but whose pen name was Goho. There was at the time a man called Oribe, the chieftain of a village on the west coast, who was quite well-versed in Chinese. Thus, upon meeting Goho he conversed with him by writing Chinese words on the sand with his cane. He wrote: "Those passengers on the ship — of what country are they? Why do they appear so different?" Goho wrote in answer: "They are traders from among the south-western barbarians. They know something of the etiquette of monarchs and ministers, but they do not know that polite attitudes are part of etiquette. Thus, when they drink, they do not exchange cups. When they eat they use their hands, not chopsticks. They know how to gratify their appetites but they cannot state their reasons in writing. These traders visit the same places in the hope of exchanging what they have for what they do not have. There is nothing suspicious about them."

Then Oribe wrote: "About 13 *ri* from here there is a seaport called Akaogi where the family to whom I owe allegiance has lived for generations. The population of the seaport is several tens of thousands of households. The people are rich and prosperous, and merchants from the south and traders from the north come and go continuously. Now this ship is anchored here, but it is far better there as the port is deep and calm." When the report of the foreign ship was made to my grandfather and to my aged father, the latter sent several tens of junks to fetch the ship at Akaogi, where it arrived on the 27th.

At that time there lived at the port a certain Zen student of senior grade. . . . Well-versed in the scriptures and the classics, he was capable of writing fast and intelligently. He met Goho with whom he carried on conversation through the written word. Goho regarded him as a true friend in an alien land — a case of like attracting like. [He reported:]

"There are two leaders among the traders, the one called Murashusa, and the other Christian Mota. In their hands they carried something two or three feet long, straight on the outside with a passage inside, and made of a heavy substance. The inner passage runs through it although it is closed at the end. At its side there is an aperture which is the passageway for fire. Its shape defies comparison with anything I know. To use it, fill it with powder and small lead pellets. Set up a small white target on a bank. Grip the object in your hand, compose your body, and closing one eye, apply fire to the aperture. Then the pellet hits the target squarely. The explosion is like lightning and the report like thunder. Bystanders must cover their ears. . . . This thing with one blow can smash a mountain of silver and a wall of iron. If one sought to do mischief in another man's domain and he was touched by it, he would lose his life instantly. Needless to say this is also true for the deer and stag that ravage the plants in the fields."

Lord Tokitaka saw it and thought it was the wonder of wonders. He did not know its name at first nor the details of its use. Then someone called it "iron-arms," although it was not known whether the Chinese called it so, or whether it was so called only on our island. . . . That year the festival day of the Ninth

his bride from among the girls of the "five families" descending from the Fugiwaras. This permanently forestalled the danger that a clever policy of marriages might put the shogunate at the mercy of the emperor.

The regime set up by Ieyasu was made still more secure under his successors, all members of the Tokugawa family, which governed the country for some 250 years, until the second half of the nineteenth century. A regime more bureaucratic and police-like than military kept the nation in a state of undisturbed order, opening up a lengthy period that is known, in fact, as "the great peace." Justification and an ideological regimen for the regime was found in the morals of Confucius, which, together with the doctrinaire elaborations of the Chinese philosophers Chu Hsi (1130–1200) and Wang Yang-ming (1472–1528), were considered the basis for the civil, familial, and social order of Japan. They educated the people of the country to obedience and submission. Neo-Confucianism also influenced the method of government; in formulations made by Fujiwara Seika (1561–1619) and Hayashi Razan (1583–1657), it became the basis of the moral code of the state, and served to order the country's administrative and political life. Order was made the categorical basis of human institutions; the social classes were considered immutable; man was valid only insofar as he carried out the norms of the state.

Social life, however, was neither as rigorous nor as conservative as politics during the Tokugawa period. With the period of internal struggles at an end, the economy flourished; new industries sprang up, cities and markets grew, and large amounts of capital came into the hands of a middle class that in certain ways was similar to the bourgeoisie of the West. Developments in engineering made possible the accomplishment of draining operations, the building of dams, underground canals, aqueducts, and bridges, the construction of new cities and villages in new areas of the country that were being opened up, particularly in the east and the north. These colossal undertakings paved the way, among other things, for the birth of Edo and the development of the entire Kanto region, which had been almost completely neglected from the time of Kamakura on.

It is not easy to assess the importance of the contribution made by the first Europeans to this renewal of Japanese life and culture. The Portuguese merchants of 1543–44 were followed by Jesuit missionaries. Francesco Saverio (1506–1554) and then Alessandro Valignano (1539–1606) undertook the preaching of the Christian religion in the country with some success and introduced the knowledge of the achievements of Western civilization. The missionaries that followed them built churches, supervised the first printed editions of texts in Latin letters, improved printing techniques, and translated a number of European literary works. But the encounter was unfortunately too ephemeral to bear lasting fruit. At the beginning of the seventeenth century, persecutions against Christianity raged in the country and suddenly cut off the cultural dialogue between the West and East, which had been pregnant with promise.

The Japanese appreciation of Christianity as the vehicle of a superior civilization, and the conduct of the Catholic missionaries, admirable when compared to the corruption rampant among the indigenous Buddhist clergy of the time, were the factors that at first had assured a great deal of sympathy for the new faith. They created a favorable terrain for the work of propagation. But other elements played an important role in the Japanese response, especially the desire for commercial and political gain. The feudal lords had often been prompted to permit and facilitate the work of conversion in their territories, in the hope that a favorable attitude toward Christianity would pay off in terms of preference and favors from the Portuguese or Spanish merchants. Hideyoshi himself had entertained the hope of obtaining a certain number of ships from the West for his military expedition to Korea. The disappointment he felt when he found out that his

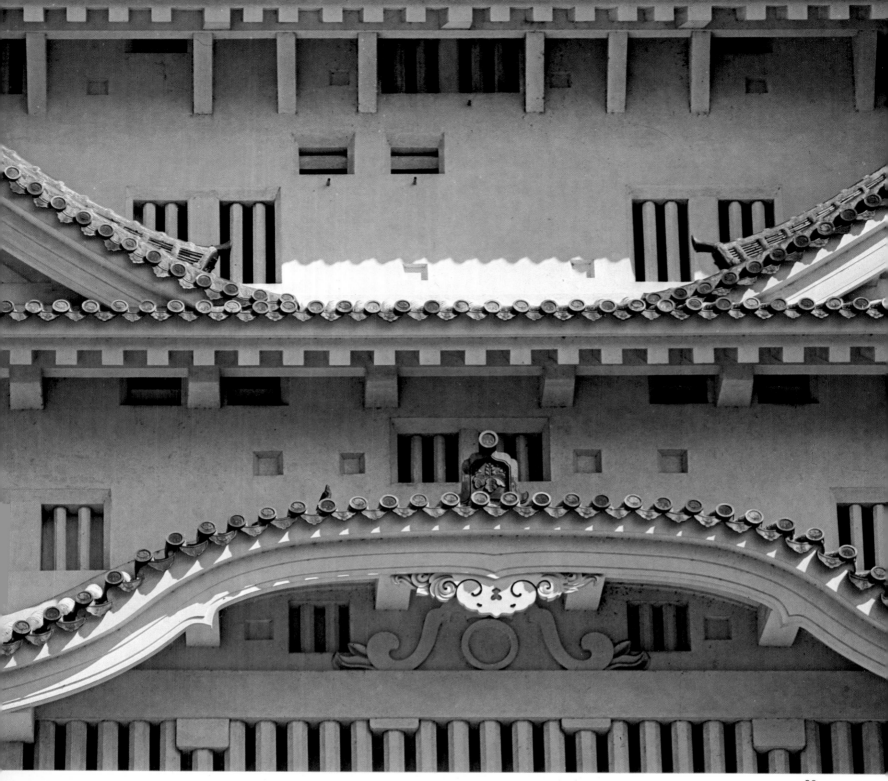

request could not be granted is thought to be one of the initial causes of his embitterment against Christianity.

Whether or not this is true, it is an established fact that in 1587 he handed down his first decree of proscription against the new religion. Then in 1596 Francisco de Olandia, the pilot of a Spanish galleon thrown onto the coast of the island of Shikoku by a storm, appears to have gone so far as to say that the King of Spain used missionaries as a vanguard to conquer the world. Tradition has it that his words, passed on to Hideyoshi, caused the first death sentences against the Christians. In the following year, in Nagasaki, 23 persons were executed. The Tokugawas continued these bans and bloody persecutions, to the point of prohibiting completely not only the preaching of Christianity but all contacts with the Nanban, (the foreigners from the south), as the Japanese now called the Westerners, who put in at the ports of the archipelago by coming up the coasts of the Indian Ocean and the Pacific. The Dutch were an exception. They were permitted to run a trade center on the island of Deshima, after William Adams

Month fell on the day of the Metal and the Boar. Thus, one fine morning the weapon was filled with powder and lead pellets, a target was set up more than a hundred paces away, and fire was applied to the weapon. At first the people were astonished; then they became frightened. But in the end they all said in unison: "We should like to learn!" Disregarding the high price of the arms, Tokitaka purchased from the aliens two pieces of the firearms for his family treasure. As for the art of grinding, sifting, and mixing of the powder, Tokitaka let his retainer, Shinokawa Shoshiro, learn it. Tokitaka occupied himself, morning and night, and without rest in handling the arms. As a result, he was able to convert the misses of his early experiments into hits — a hundred hits in a hundred attempts. . . .

So interested was Tokitaka in the weapon that he had a number of iron-workers examine and study it for months and from season to season in order to manufacture some.

Tsunoda *et al: Sources* (*pp.* 308–11)

90

89. Detail from the facade of the White Heron castle of Himeji. The work adopts building techniques, columns and capitals of a probable Occidental derivation. A.D. 1609 (Edo, or Tokugawa, Period). Himeji, Prefecture of Hyogo.

90. Detail from the enclosure wall of the Himeji castle, with two types of loopholes. A.D. 1609 (Edo Period). Himeji, Prefecture of Hyogo.

(1574–1620) managed to overcome the diffidence of Ieyasu, gaining his goodwill and esteem to the point of being hired as an expert sailor and shipbuilder.

Castles

The most conspicuous material contribution of the West to Japan remained at first that of firearms, which revolutionized military strategy. Their initial effect was to alter defensive conditions. Fortresses, which before had had to answer to the needs of sieges and were thus built as a rule in elevated positions, were now built in flat areas as well, but with structures capable of resisting firearms. At times European castles served as models or inspiration. The result was that a number of fortresses were a curious mixture of elements from local tradition with others of European origin. The structures became larger,

91. The pediment of the portal in the *ninomaru*, the middle fortress of the Nijo castle. A.D. 1626 (Edo Period). Kyoto.

Following pages:
92. Detail of the entrance portico in the Toshogu sanctuary-mausoleum, built in honor of the shogun Tokugawa Ieyasu. A.D. 1634–1636 (Edo, or Tokugawa, Period). Nikko, Prefecture of Tochigi.

Elevation of the Okayama castle, in the Prefecture of Okayama. Beginning of the seventeenth century (Edo, or Tokugawa, Period). This building was destroyed during the Second World War.

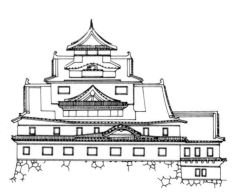

and they were reinforced with wide foundations and thick walls. They had high towers and were surrounded by deep moats. Groups of buildings with several floors, each one smaller than the other, were constructed in wood and masonry.

The castle of Matsumoto (Figure 85), in the prefecture of Nagano, was built between 1594 and 1597 on a massive stone foundation like the trunk of a pyramid. The roofs of the buildings are simple and built with sharp slopes, to handle the frequent snows in the region. The castle is composed of two large buildings conceived as guard towers, connected by a covered corridor. The importance of the thick walls can be seen even more clearly in the partial view (Figure 86), which shows the detail of the juncture between building and foundation of the castle of Kumamoto, also in Nagano prefecture, built in 1607. A dense sequence of projecting beams composes the framework that supports the wooden and masonry structures of the complex of buildings (details of which may be seen in Figures 87 and 88). The contrast between the masonry structures and those in wood is to be seen once again here, in the varied colors and textures of the different elements. The arched roofs with double slopes at times form gables with the horizontal shelter structures on each floor; the motif of the open shutters of the windows is found in both. This decorative effect is prevalent also in the castle of the White Heron of Himeji, which is the only castle still existing in its entirety. It was originally built by Toyotomi Hideyoshi and was enlarged in 1609 with four towers connected by narrow passageways with turrets. Built of stone and masonry, it is interesting for a number of minor innovations, such as the windows of the grille, which has columns both with and without capitals (Figure 89), and the loopholes in the walls (Figure 90), in forms that call to mind similar defensive structures in Western buildings.

In Japan, however, this hybrid architectural style was elaborated almost at once into the classical type of palace architecture. One of the most eloquent examples of this is to be seen in the castle of Nijo, built in Kyoto in 1602. Over a period of only a little more than twenty years, the original construction was almost completely changed, although the three circles of walls and moats, which marked the confines of the three fortresses, remained. In the innermost of these, called the *honmaru*, were the residential quarters, in a complex of buildings arranged around a large central tower. Their architecture disposes of the impression that all castle buildings must lean together to form a sort of pyramid. Although they all were projected on the same sort of plan as the earlier castles had, the buildings of Nijo were distributed over a wide area, part of which was set aside for gardens. Their monumental look is due as much to Chinese taste as it is to any supposed strength and solidity of the structures; the effect of solidity was entrusted to the ponderous cornices and gables of the roofs, which were elaborately decorated with metallic and wooden elements, in arabesques and transparent and carved compositions. Figure 91 shows the portal of the ninomaru (the "halfway fortress" of the Nijo castle), which has survived to the present day. The castle's tower and the buildings of the first series of walls have all been destroyed.

The convergence of the architecture of the castle with the classical architecture of palaces was possible in a city like Kyoto, where a long architectural tradition led in this direction. But in the other regions of Japan the process was more difficult; even when there was no longer a reason for the castles because of the changed political climate, the appearance of the early fortifications was not changed. On the other hand, the brief period of time in which all these buildings were erected assured that there would be little or no stylistic evolution. In substance the history of the castles involves only the thirty years running from 1580 to 1610, the last great era in the consolidation of feudal dominions. Thereafter, the Tokugawa regime brought about a weakening of the role of castles as centers of feudal power.

But if the fortresses were no longer put to use for military purposes,

93

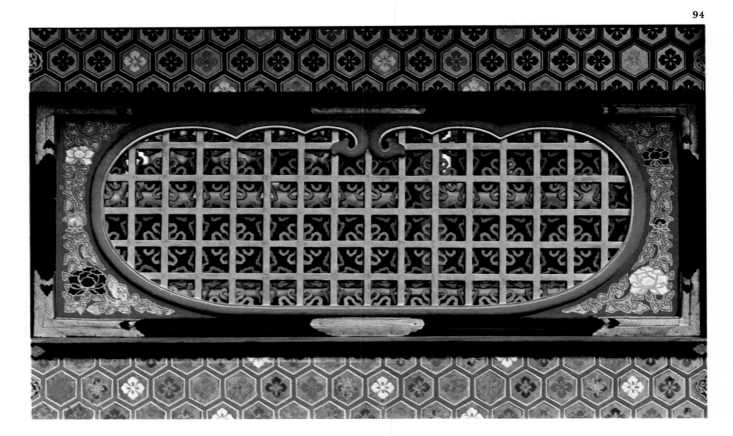

94

93. Toshogu: Detail of the entrance portico of the building, with gilded metal decoration, sculptured groups of personages, and figures of fantastic animals. A.D. 1634–1636 (Edo, or Tokugawa, Period). Nikko, Prefecture of Tochigi.

94. Toshogu: Detail of the decoration, with enamel, gilding, and arabesque and heraldic motifs. A.D. 1634–1636 (Edo Period). Nikko, Prefecture of Tochigi.

they continued to carry out an important function as economic centers. Around these, cities came into being, and in the end the country had an urban development whose elaboration satisfactorily met the needs of a central government wishing to exercise its authority over the provinces, something that had been impossible in Japan up to this time. The castles of Edo, Osaka, Sendai, and Nagoya are the basis of these cities, which are today among the most important in the Japanese economy. First, military garrisons established themselves in the vicinity of the castles; following them came industries and trading centers, temples and sanctuaries, and in a short time the feudal fortresses had been transformed into centers of production and commerce. The attraction of these centers to the inhabitants of the rural areas paved the way for truly wide-scale urban development, and the improvement in living conditions and the peaceful situation of the country had the effect of a stimulating population growth. In little more than two centuries, from 1553 to 1780, the population of Japan doubled, rising from approximately thirteen million to twenty-six million.

The Edo Epoch

The most imposing and impregnable fortress in the nation remains the castle that Tokugawa Iyeasu had built at Edo, which became the headquarters of the shogunate. Inside the spacious bastions, the various feudal lords built their homes. The city that grew up around this grandiose complex became the largest in the country and was not only the center of administration, but the very heart of the nation, with a network of roads and navigable canals that assured communication with the most remote city-castles in the land. The exceptional expansion of the urban centers — in 1700 Edo itself had more than a million inhabitants — gave an impetus to building and to the arts. New temples were erected, and the styles of residential architecture were renewed. The patronage given to Buddhism by the Tokugawas paved the way for the construction of numerous religious buildings in the capital itself as well as in the most peripheral centers, where the individual *daimyo*, following the example of the shogun, encouraged the building of new temples. The most important monastery in this period was the Keneiji of Ueno, founded by the Tendai sect.

The Tokugawas consolidated their prestige not only by their patronage of the arts and of Buddhist and Shinto institutions but also by the deification of their own line. Along the lines of the neo-Confucianism of Wang Yang-ming, Ieyasu was deified at his death with the title of Toshodai-gongen, that is, "incarnation of Buddha, great sun of the East," and became a figure of the official religion. His remains, buried in 1616 on Mount Kuno, in the prefecture of Shizuoka, were later exhumed and definitively entombed on Mount Nikko, in the sanctuary-mausoleum of Toshogu, completed between 1634 and 1636. From that time on every shogun led a state pilgrimage to Nikko, in which the *daimyos* and their retinues took part. Later, other mausoleums were built on Mount Nikko, the so-called *otamayas*, which were half tombs, half temples, dedicated to ancestors. Since the *otamayas* could not be assigned as an institution to any religion in particular, they were taken under the wing of the tolerant Shinto cult; the *otamayas* were built in forms that closely resembled the traditional Shinto sanctuaries, except for their ponderous monumentality which was obviously due to the influence of the Chinese architecture of the Ming period (1368–1644), evident even in the gables and brick porticoes. The structures, moreover, were subject to a certain European influence: there are pairs of internal vaults and columns with convex grooves.

On the portico of the Toshogu's entrance (Figure 92), the excessive profusion of sculptures and reliefs of dragons and other fantastic animals, of floral and heraldic motifs, of human figures in the garb of suppliants, throws a clear light on the new tendencies in architectural decoration. Generally speaking there is a connection with the *ninomaru* type of architecture (Figure 91), but whereas in the earlier building the decorative element is still linked primarily to the Japanese figurative repertory, in the Toshogu very little remains of the native traditions. The detail of the decoration (Figure 93) shows heavy gilt metals clearly based on Chinese models, especially in the groups of personages and in the figures of mythical animals. Figure 94 calls to mind artistic elements beyond the confines of Asia itself: the use of multicolored enamels, floral motifs following one another within regular hexagons of various colors, transparent ornamentation within the finely shaped oval — all these suggest links with Islamic art.

A more typically Japanese architecture is to be seen in the Buddhist temples, whose chief examples are to be found today among the restored buildings of the ancient temples or those added to the ancient complexes. An extremely simple and unadorned structure is that of the Daishido, in the Jingoji, erected at the end of the sixteenth century (Figure 95). Dating back to the same period — but richer, almost residential, though light in its structure — is the Shoshinden of the Daigakuji in Kyoto, (already illustrated in Figure 41). There are only a few innovations. For the most part the monuments conform with tradition, "contaminating" one or more suggestions from the ancient *shinden-zukuri* with architectural elements of the *chado* and the *shoin* style. In 1600 the golden hall of the Onjoji was built. Figure 96 shows this in a partial view with an access stairway and the ritual stone lantern in the center of the clearing in front of the temple. The construction of the main building (konpon-chudo) of the Enryakuji in the

SENNO KUDEN ON IKEBANA

I have so many leisurely hours here at my hermitage I entertain myself by gathering some old tree branches and by putting them in a cracked jar. As I sit watching them, various thoughts come to my mind. Mount Lu and Lake Hsiang are said to be scenic, but we cannot enjoy the beauty unless we go there. The jade trees and fairy pond in the Kunlung Mountains are famous, but they are rarely to be seen. Even Wang Wei's painting of the Wang River cannot produce a cool breeze of summer; even Ch'ien Hsüan's scroll depicting flowers cannot yield the fragrance of autumn. We shall have to labor ourselves a good deal to build a rock garden or a water fountain in our frontyard. In contrast, floral art can represent a vast scene of mountains and rivers with just a little water and small twigs; it can give a great variety of amusement within a brief period of time. It may rightly be called a miracle-worker's art. A certain poet of antiquity had his lover sleep on the seven parts of a mat, himself lying on the remaining three. Likewise I put my flower vase on the seven and myself on the three, whereupon the alcove becomes so fascinating that I am never tired of looking at it. I feel as if I were not far away from the jewelry trees and treasure ponds of Paradise, as I smell above the vase a breeze from a divine world. Buddha himself, from his earliest teachings to his most mature, has consistently taught in terms of flowers. Don't the colors blue, yellow, red, white, and black represent the Five Faculties and the Five Parts? The death of numerous flowers in winter reveals the law of change and mutability in life, too, and if in that desolate scene there is a patch of land with pine and cedar trees, that would symbolize the eternal truth of the cosmos. When Buddha was asked to give a sermon on Vulture Peak, he simply showed a flower to the audience as he turned it in his fingers. Among the people who watched, Kashyapa alone understood the meaning and smiled. Buddha's intuitive experience of the Right Law and Enlightenment, not expressible in words, was thus transmitted from one heart to another, and Buddha praised the disciple's high attainment. Hsieh Ling-yün reached the stage of enlightenment as he watched peach blossoms; so did Huang Shan-ku as he smelled the fragrance of Asian olive blossoms. A person who arranges flowers can not only entertain himself amid the plants of nature that change with the seasons; he might, as he watches flowers and leaves falling, hit upon an invaluable clue to enlightenment, too.

Weda: *Literary and Art Theories* (*pp.* 81–83) Page 158 top and center

95

95. Jingoji: The Daishido building. (Momoyama Period). Kyoto.

prefecture of Shiga, dates back to 1640; figure 97 shows the upper part of it, with the particularly broad slope of the roof.

The masterpieces of the architecture of this epoch, however, are two groups of buildings which were for residential, not religious, use: the Katsura and Shugakuin villas, built in isolated positions in the surroundings of Kyoto in the first half of the seventeenth century. The imperial villa of Katsura (Figure 98 shows a view from above, including its lake) is distinguished by the simplicity of the line of the various buildings, the balance of their proportions, the use of woods left in their natural state, the lovely effect of merging with the surrounding garden. Figure 99 shows the pavilion in the garden, overlooking the lake, which fits in perfectly with the luxuriant vegetation of the background and the soft colors of the water and the lawn. The Katsura villa exhibits perhaps the finest synthesis of Japanese garden art, which unites in harmonious fashion the elements of a landscape no longer that of the wild and mountainous type, but of a gentler, more cheerful and country-like sort, in line with the concept introduced by Sen no Rikyu (1521–1591), a well-known designer of gardens and master of the tea ceremony.

Architecture and Art of the Tokugawa

The growth of the cities in the time of the Tokugawa paved the way not only for great nobles' residences but for civic building activity, which involved the more modest homes of other classes. The dwindling amount of building area made it increasingly necessary to add a second floor to Japanese houses, but third floors were rare. Homes were usually built on platforms raised two or three feet above the ground; their posts were erected on stone foundations, which supported the wooden floors and the pillars, also wood, that made up the framework of the buildings. The outer walls were built of masonry and plaster, at least on two sides. The other two sides had sliding walls or particularly large windows opening onto verandas. The roof, invariably reinforced by wooden beams, was covered with tiles. The interior was divided into a number of rooms by the use of sliding walls and screens. The ever more extensive use of *tatami* mats, approximately three feet by six in size, dictated the spacing and arrangement of the inner pillars of the buildings. The arrangements were no longer calculated on the basis of the distance between the centers of the pillars, but rather on the actual space between one pillar and the other. A greater freedom in planning, especially in the distribution of the rooms, was obtained by placing the structural members close to the edges of the building or in the corner, in order to leave the inner rooms as empty as possible. This resulted in a most complex framework for the roofs, which had to make up for the lack of support at the building's center. This was one of the reasons, together with the frequency of earthquakes and fires, for imposing a height limit on buildings, which in more recent times was fixed at 101 feet 8 inches for monumental edifices (compared to the approximately 311 feet 7 inches reached in ancient times by the pagoda of the Todaiji, the tallest building in all Japanese architecture). Because of the use of wood, the architecture was also governed in its dimensions by the average length of the trees from which the individual building elements were made.

The essential lines of this civic building activity combined simplicity with stunning spatial effects and gave rise to the so-called *sukiya* style, which crowned the evolution of Japanese residential architecture, establishing the type of dwelling to which the traditional Japanese home of the present day remains closely tied. A striking example of this is to be seen in the seventeenth-century home of Yoshimura, in the prefecture of Osaka (Figure 100) and in Kyoto residences of the seventeenth and eighteenth centuries (Figures 101 and 102). The elaborate and careful processing of the wood gives this architecture the appearance of fine cabinetwork. Windows with gratings and low enclosing fences are still typical of the private homes in Kyoto. Figure 101 shows the facade of an ancient vacation home of Shimabara with an adjacent restaurant built about 1640 and then partially rebuilt in 1787. Despite the use for which the later rebuilding had been planned, it does not differ a great deal from the residential architecture of the same period.

The development of new building techniques in the cities was accompanied by an increase in the related industries and arts, so that furnishings could be even more comfortable and refined. There are innumerable examples of rare beauty of this sort; the grillwork of windows with highly luminous effects and sharp contrasts between black and white (Figure 103); the decorations of inner rooms and doors, like that of the home of Yoshimura, with painted branches and leaves (Figure 104). Among the most popular kinds of furnishings were small items of furniture, screens, lacquer articles, and pottery.

Famous artists such as Ogata Korin (1658–1716) were not above

AESTHETICS AS ENUNCIATED BY BASHO

There is a common element permeating Saigyo's lyric poetry, Sogi's linked verse, Sesshu's painting, and Rikyu's tea ceremony. It is the poetic spirit, the spirit that leads one to follow the ways of the universe and to become a friend with things of the seasons. For a person who has the spirit, everything he sees becomes a flower and everything he imagines turns into a moon. Those who do not see the flower are no different from barbarians, and those who do not imagine the flower are akin to beasts. Leave barbarians and beasts behind; follow the ways of the universe and return to nature.

The Master [Basho] said: "Learn about a pine tree from a pine tree, and about a bamboo plant from a bamboo plant." What he meant was that the poet should detach the mind from his own self. Nevertheless some people interpret the word "learn" in their own ways and never really "learn." "Learn" means to enter into the object, perceive its delicate life, and feel its feeling, whereupon a poem forms itself. Even a poem that lucidly describes an object could not attain a true poetic sentiment unless it contains the feelings that spontaneously emerged out of the object. In such a poem the object and the poet's self would remain forever separate for it was composed by the poet's personal self.

Weda: *Literary and Art Theories* (*pp.* 147–48, 157–58)

Plan, elevation, and transverse section of the reading hall of the Enryakuji.

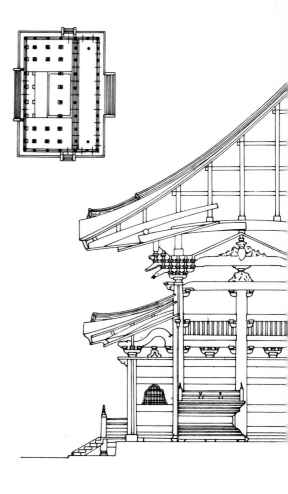

96. Onjoji: Access stairway to the golden hall of the temple. A.D. 1600 (Momoyama Period). Onjoji-machi, Otsu, Prefecture of Shiga.

Following pages:

97. Enryakuji. Detail from the large sloping roof of the main temple building, known as the Konpon-chudo, equivalent to the golden hall. A.D. 1640 (Edo, or Tokugawa, Period). Sakamoto, Otsu, Prefecture of Shiga.

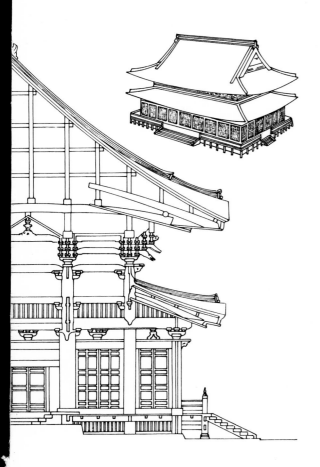

using their talents to decorate humble anonymous objects of everyday use, thus becoming the precursors, so to speak, of the designers of the present day. The great Japanese pictorial tradition continued, meanwhile, with the artists of the Kano and Tosa schools, whose works were commissioned to adorn and decorate the interiors of more sumptuous dwellings. The urge to display wealth and taste paved the way for a wide variety of paintings on panels, sliding walls, and screens. The polychrome *yamato-e* was fused with the severe technique of the *sumi-e*, or "ink paintings," combining the luminosity of color with the vigor of the brush stroke to produce extraordinary effects of splendor and grandeur. A repertory of landscapes, flowers, and birds, sometimes based on the Chinese art of the Ming period, decorated the so-called blue and gold screens. The painting of the Bridge of Uji (Figure 105), from the end of the sixteenth century or the outset of the seventeenth century, belongs to this type of decoration as does the Moon Landscape (Figure 107) attributed to Tosa Mitsuyoshi (1539–1613). A number of styles, from the most abstract symbolism to the most graphic realism, make up a genre that is dazzling with color, gold, and light, evoking in us perhaps the Spanish baroque of the sixteenth century, with its vivid colors and sharp tonal contrasts.

A direct reference to the Western world is to be found in the painting of the so-called *nanban-byobu*, the "screens of the foreigners from the south." In a sumptuous style, though sometimes awkward in their depiction of unfamiliar objects, a great variety of European subjects is represented: sailing vessels, merchants, missionaries, musical instruments, even landscapes and types of architecture, often set in the Arcadian atmosphere typical of the European painting of the sixteenth and seventeenth centuries. One of these paintings (Figure 106) reproduces with curious detail a high-ranking Portuguese with his entourage. The black man holding the umbrella, the dog on a leash, the clothing depicted with absolute precision, the exaggerated and amusing physical features (the large nose, for example), are eloquent examples of the spirit of observation and interest the Japanese accorded the first Europeans to land on their coasts. But the screens were a page in the artistic history of Japan that had little sequel; production of such works necessarily came to an end when all ties with the West were broken off.

Beginning of the Modern Era

Japan was closed off to foreigners once and for all in 1639. Motivated by political and religious considerations, the ban ended by disrupting relations between the archipelago and Europe. The only precarious point of contact was Deshima, a small island in the port of Nagasaki, where the Dutch managed, in the face of considerable difficulties, to maintain a monopoly on foreign trade. They were authorized to spread certain elements of European culture, primarily of a scientific and medical nature. Interest in such matters had not quite been suffocated by the weight of anti-Christian prejudices. European culture from this time on was called *rangaku*, "the science of the Dutch." There has as yet been no thorough study of the contribution made by the new ideas to the internal renewal of the nation, but there is no question that the comparison between Western scientific and speculative achievements and those of either the indigenous tradition or that of Chinese neo-Confucianism were effective in stimulating the reassessment of theories of society and of the nation which took place in these centuries.

The penetration of Western culture had introduced a new concept of man and his relations with society and the state. The Tokugawas feared, as had Hideyoshi before them, that Christianity was but the shadow of a nation seeking conquest and that a coalition of Catholic feudatories might even put the nation at the mercy of some foreign state. The chief reason for opposing the new religion, however, was the profoundly revolutionary value of its teaching, its ideas of equality and freedom of the

spirit. There would otherwise be no explanation for the fact that a personality like Arai Hakuseki (1657–1725) was assigned to bring to trial the humble Italian missionary Giovanni Battista Sidotti (1668–1715), who was guilty of having entered Japan illegally. The persecutions unleashed between 1597 and 1614 reduced the number of Christians from three-hundred thousand to only a few thousand, and put an end to proselytizing activity throughout the country. From that time on, small communities of Christians, the well-known occult Christians, handed the faith down from generation to generation without any ecclesiastic organization whatever, up until the time the country reopened its borders to the West.

This reopening occurred in the middle of the nineteenth century. For some time the Western powers brought pressure to bear to make Japan abandon its isolation and open its ports to the black ships. In 1853 Commodore Matthew C. Perry, at the command of a special United States naval expedition, entered the Bay of Edo with a message from President Millard Fillmore requesting the reopening of Japan. This and other threatening moves dissuaded Japan from responding with a refusal, and the following year it ratified its first international treaty with the United States, Russia, Great Britain, and Holland. The event triggered a series of domestic upheavals that precipitated the fall of the Tokugawa shogunate. In 1867 authentic power was placed in

98. View from above of the residential complex and lake of the Katsura imperial villa. First half of the seventeenth century A.D. (Edo, or Tokugawa, Period). Kyoto.

99. The garden pavilion of the Katsura imperial villa, with its lake and rocks. First half of the seventeenth century A.D. (Edo, or Tokugawa, Period). Kyoto.

Following pages:

100. Detail from the facade of the house of Yoshimura, a building typical of seventeenth-century A.D. residential architecture. (Edo, or Tokugawa, Period). Prefecture of Osaka.

the hands of the young Emperor Mutsuhito who, in rising to the throne with the name of Meiji, revamped the empire, transferring the court to Edo. He renamed the city Tokyo, (the capital of the East), and made it the new imperial seat. Promulgating a constitution that set up a constitutional monarchy, the new emperor pursued policies aimed at transforming the nation into a modern state organized along European lines. Over a period of only a few years the country underwent such sweeping changes that soon very little remained of the ancient feudal culture, or at least of the manners and aspects that had been typical of it.

Growth of a New Philosophy

Japanese feudal culture had gone through a considerable change, however, in the two centuries in which the country was closed to the outside world. The new philosophy went far beyond the bounds of pure speculative abstraction and plunged into an analysis of economics and politics with surprising urgency. Scholars worked out their earliest theories on a basis of Confucian-type assessments. The Japanese had been profoundly influenced by the Chinese concept of the mythical Golden Age, after which all history was purported to be a retrogression, in moral and social terms. The Confucian ideal of antiquity had stirred up in the souls of the erudite Japanese a new veneration for their own past, and had made them entertain the dream of a return to the purity of their origins, to the primitive institutions of their fatherland. The process was a slow and gradual one that from the movement of the *kangakusha* (the sinologists), champions of Chinese culture, advanced through a thousand nuances to the attitude of the *kokugakusha* (or *wagakusha*), the "yamatologists," who supported the original national culture and spirit of Japan. The movement of the *kangakusha*, eminently literary and philosophical, had in effect promoted a large-scale dissemination in Japan of Chinese culture, above all of neo-Confucianism. But indications are that, in the end, the indiscriminate exaltation of Chinese culture brought about a heated reaction that led to a reevaluation of the indigenous cultural heritage. And yet the movement of the *kokugakusha*, which in fact stands for "those dedicated to national studies," was successful less as an opposing force than as a promoter of ideas following the same lines of development as those promoted by the *kangakusha*. It was only logical that once the Chinese myth of the Golden Age was brought forward again, the Japanese should seek traces of such an age in their own historical and religious tradition, in order to draw from the source of exemplary moral and political conduct. The Meiji restoration of 1868 was really the fruit of this progressive reawakening.

In point of fact, during the entire period of Tokugawa rule, Japanese culture showed an effort to adapt the results of the Chinese experience to realistic national needs. For a time, of course, this effort was oriented toward the assimilation of the achievements of European civilization. The stimuli and ferment of ideas imported from abroad might have sparked a sudden evolution in the archipelago's feudal structure itself, just as the development of production and mercantilism had already promised to do after the first half of the sixteenth century. But the Tokugawa regime had set up policies restricting commerce and bolstering feudal controls, so that the impulse given by the new activity was unable to expand. The economic explosion was prevented by the legal impediment from going beyond the confines of the archipelago. The thick curtain that had been lowered made the nation impenetrable. The political and social atmosphere became suffocating, and the rigid division of the feudal society into classes increased the unease.

The official hierarchy saw the military in the front ranks, followed by the farmers, the artisans, and lastly the merchants. The particularly low position to which the merchants were relegated, listed only one rung above the pariahs (the *eta*), was the grievous legacy of a typically Chinese and Confucian concept of life and thought, which considered

101. Detail from the facade of a luxury residence of the seventeenth or eighteenth century A.D. (Edo, or Tokugawa, Period). Kyoto.

102. The corner of a typical luxury house of the seventeenth and eighteenth centuries A.D. (Edo, or Tokugawa, Period). Kyoto.

CHIKAMATSU ON REALISM

"In writing *joruri*, [puppet plays] one attempts first to describe facts as they really are, but in so doing one writes things which are not true, in the interest of art. To be precise, many things are said by the female characters which real women could not utter. Such things fall under the heading of art; it is because they say what could not come from a real woman's lips that their true emotions are disclosed. If in such cases the author were to model his character on the ways of a real woman and conceal her feelings, such realism, far from being admired, would permit no pleasure in the work. Thus, if one examines a play without paying attention to the question of art, one will probably criticize it on the grounds that it contains many unpleasant words which are not suitable for women. But such things should be considered as art. In addition, there are numerous instances in the portrayal of a villain as excessively cowardly, or of a clown as being funny, which are outside the truth and which must be regarded as art. The spectator must bear this consideration in mind. . . . Art is something which lies in the slender margin between the real and the unreal. Of course it seems desirable, in view of the current taste for realism, to have the chief retainer in the [*Kabuki*] play copy the gestures and speech of a real retainer, but in that case should a real chief retainer of a daimyo put rouge and powder on his face like an actor? Or, would it prove entertaining if an actor, on the grounds that real chief retainers do not make up their faces, were to appear on the stage and perform, with his beard growing wild and his head shaven? This is what I mean by the slender margin between the real and the unreal. It is unreal, and yet it is not unreal; it is real, and yet it is not real. Entertainment lies between the two.

Tsunoda *et al: Sources* (*pp.* 438–39)

commerce the most despicable and corrupt of activities, since it produced nothing and its only end was personal gain. But the development of a monetary economy, which the Tokugawas themselves had favored by minting gold and silver coins, necessarily gave the merchant class greater power, and the neo-Confucian philosophers themselves began to consider trade in a more positive spirit, and looked on it with more benevolent eyes. The writer Ishada Baigan (1685–1744), who lived in contact with commercial circles of Kyoto and Osaka, lifted an authoritative voice in defense of the merchants. Far from accepting neo-Confucian ideological conditioning, the merchants progressively consolidated their positions. They not only accumulated wealth, but they imposed a new taste in life and gave rise to a new culture, which was that of the so-called *chomin* (the common people).

The sectors in which this new culture expressed itself most completely were those of literature and the arts. Narrative, rather than drawing its subjects from the great deeds of illustrious men as before, began to draw them from everyday life. It related the vicissitudes of the man on the street. The novels of Ibara Saikaku (1642–1693) and Ejima Kiseki (1677–1736), who were the writers most in vogue at the time, faithfully mirrored with realistic descriptions the contemporary society of the common people. The novels *Koshoku Ichidai Onna* ("A Courtesan")

THE PRINCIPLES OF PAINTING ACCORDING TO MITSUOKI

"The spirit's circulation" means that the painter, as he sets out to work, lets the spirit of his soul circulate through his body. When his soul is small and his spirit insufficient, his brushwork will be stunted, feeble, and always unsatisfactory. The painter's brushwork should become gentle and soft upon grief, coarse and strong upon anger, mellow and carefree upon joy; it is essential that the painter choose the precise emotion. . . . "Life's motion" means that a painting, whether of a god or a devil or a man, whether of a beast or a bird or a tree, contains the spirit of the object and thereby makes the spectator feel as if the object were standing before his eyes. A warrior should show his martial glory, a court lady her elegant charm, a Buddhist priest an appearance of his holy mission. A bird should have the force of soaring and singing, a beast the vigor of howling and scampering. A pine or cypress tree should show the mysteriously venerable shape with which it stands through the snow and frost; a dragon or a tiger should display the force by which it catches the spirit of the wind and the clouds, moving even heaven and earth. . . .

Particularly important is the case of painting men and human life. Unless the painting

successfully transmits the spirit of the object, it will have nothing divine in it, and, if that is the case, the work is like a shrine with no god in it. No ordinary artist can transmit such a spirit into his work; . . . there would be no need for talking about principles of painting, if painting were no more than an art of copying the shape. The ultimate aim of painting is to represent the spirit of the object. In every work of painting, whether it is of human life, a bird, a beast, an insect, or a fish, the spirit of a living object can be represented only by putting eyes into the painting. A portrait, whatever fine complexion or shapely figure it may have, will suffer from the lack of a living spirit if it is dead in the eyes.

Weda: *Literary and Art Theories* (*pp.* 136–37)

103. *Sumiya*, window grilles of eighteenth century A.D. luxury residences (Edo, or Tokugawa, Period). Kyoto.

104. The Yoshimura residence: A door with painted decorations of branch and leaf motifs. Seventeenth century A.D. (Edo, or Tokugawa, Period). Prefecture of Osaka.

of Saikaku, and *Kisei Iro Samisen* ("The Love Guitar of the Prostitutes") of Kiseki, are highly eloquent examples of a literary genre that narrates the loves of prostitutes, the adventures of ruthless individuals, the vicissitudes of businessmen in the large cities. The neighborhoods where the courtesans lived became the preferred setting of the stories that were written in this period, and novels were often based on actual events. In the works of Chikamatsu (1653–1725), who is considered the leading Japanese dramatist, business clerks come onto the scene

105. The Bridge of Uji. Decoration on a six-section screen painted with gold and color on paper: 5 feet .94 inch by 10 feet 5 inches. End of the sixteenth, beginning of the seventeenth century A.D. (Momoyama or Edo periods). (Tokyo National Museum).

as the new heroes, who spurn the duels of oldtime warriors for a no less tragic death in the company of a lover. *Sonezaki Shinju* ("The Double Suicide of Sonezaki"), a sad story of love set in a squalid pleasure district, is not only one of the most significant works of the social writings of Chikamatsu but also one of the finest works in the entire Japanese dramatic repertory. The *kabuki* theater and the theater of the marionettes, known as the *Bunraku* (or *Ningyo-shibai*), had crucial importance in this epoch in the renewal not only of popular spectacles

106. The Portuguese in Japan. Detail from a screen painting of the arrival of the first Europeans in the archipelago. About the middle of the seventeenth century A.D. (Edo, or Tokugawa, Period). (Paris Museum Guimet).

107. Moon Landscape. Painting attributed to Tosa Mitsuyoshi. Second half of the sixteenth century A.D. (Muromachi or Momoyama period). Detail from the six-section screen decoration: 4 feet 10 inches by 10 feet 3 inches. (Tokyo National Museum).

Following page:
108. Scene of common life in Kyoto: The festival of Gion. Middle of the seventeenth century A.D. (Edo, or Tokugawa, Period).

but of all dramaturgy, and it is often difficult to separate the contribution of writing from that of the theater in the development of the new realistic literature.

The same orientation is to be seen in the figurative arts, painting in particular, which gradually became aware of the human element within the social context. Figure 108 shows one of the initial works of Japanese genre painting. Dating from the middle of the seventeenth century the "Festival of Gion," depicts a procession of allegorical floats along the streets of Kyoto, with a taste for environment that does not shrink from dwelling on minor details: the personages in costumes, the spectators, the vagrants, men in their homes intent on various tasks. The painting is not only the representation of a holiday but the living portrait of a city caught in a moment of its daily life.

All in all, this is a genre that comes as a forerunner of the realism and elegance of the *ukiyo-e*, the "painting of the floating world," which with much greater vitality and intimacy was to adhere to the aesthetic ideals of the bourgeois citizenry. A wide-scale production of paintings and prints, in white and black and in colors, presented a portrait of a lively, exuberant society that was now oriented toward the Western world. Book illustrations, portraits of actors and courtesans, scenes from everyday life, and views of famous landscapes were the repertory of artists like Utamaro (1754–1806), Hokusai (1760–1849) and Hiroshige (1797–1858). Their styles, oddly enough, had great influence on Western art at the end of the nineteenth century and the beginning of the twentieth. Sent to the great international expositions held in the nineteenth century by a Japan newly interested in all the West had to offer, the *ukiyo-e* prints and paintings were the first works to be seen and admired by the modern world from a country that, long an enigma, had once and for all broken through the last of the barriers that Japan had erected to isolate itself from the mainstream of world history.

THE GROWTH OF CITIES   173

APPENDICES

JAPANESE MONUMENTS
THROUGH THE AGES

The Discovery of Japan by the West

The first authentic report of the Japanese archipelago arrived in Europe with Marco Polo (1254–1324). Marco Polo did not visit Japan, but what he heard in China of the fabulous Chipangu, or Zipagu (from the Chinese Jih-pen-kuo, the "land of the rising sun"), he depicted in a lively image in his classic, *Il Milione:*

Marco Polo: *Il Milione* "The Travels of Marco Polo"

Zipagu is an island lying in the sea to the east a thousand five hundred miles away. It is very large, and its people are white, have good manners, and are good-looking. They are idolatrous and are dominated by no one, if not by themselves. Gold is to be found here and in great quantities. Nobody goes there, no merchants take the gold away, that is why they have so much. And the palace of the lord of the island is very large and is covered with gold as in our country churches are covered with lead. And the entire floor of the rooms is covered with gold two inches thick and all the windows and walls and all other things and even the halls are covered with gold. One cannot gauge its value. They have large quantities of pearls, and they are red and round and large, and more precious than the white ones. They have many other kinds of precious stones. One cannot count all the wealth of this island.

In his book, Marco Polo did not identify this country as an archipelago, and well into the sixteenth century Europeans believed that Chipangu — or Jampon as it was also being called from the earliest Portuguese sources — was made up of only one island. Marco Polo's description appears typical of a merchant accustomed to appraise what he saw in terms of wealth. But the picture he painted of Japan was probably based on what the Chinese themselves said in the aftermath of the abortive expeditions to the archipelago sent by Kublai Khan. The plans for the conquest of Japan had probably been motivated by the Chinese leaders' desire for its treasures.

The next real information about Japan came to Europe some two centuries later with a report sent in 1513 by a Portuguese agent in Malacca, Tomé Pires by name, who had gathered his information on the islands from several Chinese:

Tomé Pires: *The Suma Oriental*

The island of Jampon, according to the Chinese, is larger than that of the Lequjos (Ryukyu) and its king is grander and more powerful. Neither he nor his subjects dedicate themselves to commerce. The king is a pagan, a vassal of the King of China. They have few contacts with China because it is a great distance away. They have no junks and they are not seamen. The Lequjos reach Jampon in seven or eight days; they carry their merchandise there and barter it for gold and copper. Everything the Lequjos wear comes from Jampon. The Lequjos trade with the local people clothing, fishing nets, and other commodities.

In 1542 or 1543, the first Portuguese actually landed on the coast of Japan. In 1547, Captain Jorge Alvarez took away from Japan an inhabitant of Kagoshima, one Yajiro. Shortly thereafter, the two of them met with Francesco Saverio, a missionary of the Society of Jesus who had been sent to the East Indies by the Pope. Saverio later described the encounter as follows:

Francesco Saverio: *Monumenta Xaveriana* "Monumenta Historica Societatis Jesu"

While I was in this city of Malacca a certain group of Portuguese merchants brought news of several extremely large islands which had only recently been discovered. According to these merchants our holy faith could harvest much fruit there, much more abundantly than in any other part of India in that the people are exceedingly desirous of learning, which is not true of these gentle Indians. Along with the merchants who came to visit me was a Japanese fellow by the name of Angero, who had heard about me from the fellows who had visited his country. . . . He knows Portuguese fairly well, so that I understand him and he understands me. . . . If all Japanese are so anxious to learn as this man, their nation, in my view, is the most singular one discovered so far.

After the initial report of Saverio, news of Japan came to the West much more frequently, throwing light not only on the problems of the missionaries' activities but also on the more significant aspects of the culture of the archipelago. Thus, one such missionary, Luis Frois, wrote about 1585:

Luis Frois: *Tratado em que contem muito susinta e abreviadamenta . . . e esta provincia de Japão.*

Many people in Europe are tall and carry themselves well; here as a rule they are very small. In our country courtesy obliges us to remove our hats; the Japanese remove their shoes. Our women bear the names of blessed saints; the names of the Japanese women are Kettle, Crane, Turtle, Sandal, Tea or Reed. Women in Europe never go out of the house without permission from their husbands; Japanese women go where they like without their husbands knowing anything about it. In sewing, European women use a copper thimble, and the Japanese women a piece of hide held in the palm of their hands or a ball of crumpled paper held between their fingers. We believe in a future reward or punishment, but the bonzos say there is nothing but birth and death. Our monasteries have iron clocks while the clocks of those in Japan run on water. Our dead are laid out on their backs; the Japanese dead are curled up with their heads between their knees. We learn the sciences and arts from books; they spend their entire lives trying to understand the intrinsic significance of their graphic signs. We fight on horseback; the Japanese dismount when they go into battle. We mount a horse with our left foot, the Japanese with the right. In our part of the world scrofula, gout, and the plague are very common, in Japan very rare. Our beds are always in their place in our bedrooms; those of the Japanese are folded up and put away during the day. For us precious stones, gold and silver are objects of value; the Japanese prefer old tea pots, cracked porcelain ware, pottery, etc. In our countries it is not so common for women to know how to write; for the Japanese women the contrary is a humiliation.

Together with such descriptions, which are largely of ethnographic value, the West began to get its first notions of Japan's religions, culture, and art. In a letter dated from 1565, the Spaniard Almeida provided an interesting summary of a visit to the castle of Tamon in Nara, built by Matsunaga Hisahide (1510–1577):

Almeida: *Cartas de Alfonso d'Alberquerque*

Since this gentleman, as I have said, was so powerful because of his wealth and lands and was scrupulously obeyed, he decided to built a fortress in this city, as is the custom in their country. With this end in mind he took possession of a hill and made the necessary excavations since the earth was soft, and erected many towers of the same material. In the center he left a large open space, about a third of the circumference of the city of Goa, and dug a number of wells, for much water was found at a depth of three arm-lengths. He then invited the highest and most powerful noblemen and those of their vassals whom he trusted to build their homes inside this space and divided up the available area. He began all this five years ago and all the noblemen and vassals, one envious of the other, built the richest and most sumptuous homes imaginable, using good heavy beams after our own fashion. All these buildings, like the outside rim of the castle and its towers, are built with the most candid and smoothest walls I have ever seen in Christianity, for they do not mix sand with their lime but a special type of very white paper they manufacture for this purpose.

All the houses and the towers are covered with the finest tiles I have ever seen. They were all colored black and manufactured in various forms, and were two inches thick. Once they were made they lasted unchanged four or five hundred years, as I myself was able to see in temples built six or seven hundred years ago. To enter this city (which is what I feel you might call it) and to walk through its streets is like being in paradise. It is so clean and candid that all the buildings appear to have been built that very day.

In my view there can hardly be a more beautiful vision in the world than this fortress as seen from the outside, in that it is an absolute joy to look at it. I went inside to see the palaces and to describe them one would need a ream of paper, because they do not seem to have been built by human hands. Not only are the buildings constructed in cedar whose fragrance is a delight to the nostrils of those who enter, but all the verandas are built with single beams some seven feet long. The walls are all decorated with paintings of ancient events on a background of golden leaves. The pillars are enclosed in lead for about a hand's length from their base and at the extremities, or gilded and carved in such a way that everything seems to be covered with gold. In the center of the pillar are marvellous knobs decorated in the same fashion. The ceiling of this edifice gives the impression that it is one sole piece of wood, since one can see no junctures, even with a careful examination. I have no words to describe the other decorations.

In 1582, the first diplomatic mission of Japanese noblemen left Japan for a visit to Pope Gregory XIII; their arrival in Italy naturally caused a great sensation in Europe, and the *Cronaca Savina*, a contemporary chronicle, reported on the country of the guests as follows:

Cronaca Savina

Japan is an island nation three times the size of Italy. It was discovered by Portuguese merchants navigating beyond eastern India between the east and the north, situated in our hemisphere (having raised the Artic Pole by some 35 degrees), but its diameter is almost the same as that of Italy. It lies in the sea that bathes the uttermost limits of Asia, which is the great kingdom of China, or Sina. The distance between the two is not quite 80 leagues by ferry. It is divided into 63 dominions, since the people there are excessively desirous of honor and of reigning, so that the princes are constantly warring in order to keep or extend their territories. They accompany the art of war with the study of religion, though they worship false gods, which explains why the provinces are full of the sumptuous and rich monasteries of their religious men, which they call Bonzos, most of whom are noblemen. But since their religion, or to be more exact superstition, is full of errors, it is only logical that there are many sects and the Bonzos compete with one another in seeking truth, which they can never find, just as the princes are forever warring over land.

The *Cronaca* adds to the above report a delightful description of the habits of the Japanese guests:

Cronaca Savina

They are particularly small in stature and are of an olive complexion. Their eyes are small, their eyelids large, their noses rather wide at the end, but of a naive, gentlemanly aspect in no way barbarous. Their manners are civil, courteous, and modest, and they are very respectful of one another even when they are out walking together. They are fairly free in their eating habits, partaking of everything on the table without waiting to be served. They are frugal and clean, touching no food with their hands except bread. They do not drink wine but a very warm water in keeping with the custom of Japan. As a rule they drink this only once toward the end of their meal. When they eat together they use certain sticks of white wood like ivory, which are sharp at the end, about a palm long and which they hold between the fingers of the right hand. They pick up any sort of food with these sticks with great ability, even if the food in question is not particularly solid. They sleep fully dressed, even when they are ill. They are clever and prudent and very shrewd; in conversing with the prelates they have such good manners that they seem to have been brought up in Italy. They take note of everything they see, but are not particularly surprised, in which they show great and noble souls. They know Portuguese well and Spanish tolerably well; they understand a good deal of Latin and have a very good knowledge of Italian. They are not always sure of themselves when speaking, however, so when they negotiate with princes they speak their own language and use an interpreter.

They know how to play the harpsichord, the cithern, the lyre, and keep all these instruments in their homes. They know how to play magic tricks and also how to dance. They wear silken garments that are extremely light, such as taffeta, materials with various highly beautiful colors with many kinds of flowers, birds and other animals of Japan. They wear short boots of a certain kind of hide that is so thin and soft that you could roll it into a ball in your hand. The boots are colored and so shiny that they appear to be of silk, all of one piece, with only one hole in which laces are tied. The foot of these boots is made like those gloves that have the thumb separated from the other fingers. The Japanese shoes are like those of the Capuchin monks, without heels, pointed in front. For vamp there is only one cord which hardly covers the points of the toes, so that those who are not used to them appear unable to walk when they have them on.

They wear a long garment of silk, which they thrust into seamen's type trousers, which reach all the way down to their heels and are united in such a way that they seem one garment and these in turn so well united with the upper garment that both together appear to be only one piece of clothing. They also wear a wide band of silk on their right shoulder and under their left arm like our soldiers. In Italy they wear hats, or berets, but in Japan itself they do not wear anything on their heads and protect themselves from the rain and the sun with umbrellas and parasols. Their scimitars are particularly well-tempered because in Japan they are not esteemed unless they will pierce any sort of armor.

Tea was discussed in the *Ragionamenti* ("Reasonings") of Francesco Carletti, a Florentine merchant who, embarking on a round-the-world trip in 1594 was in Japan in 1597–1598:

Francesco Carletti: *Ragionamenti sopra le cose vedute nei viaggi dell'-Indie Occidentalei e d'altri Paesi*

The Japanese have a certain leaf which they call *cha* or *tea* and which is produced by a plant similar to that of the box plant, except that the leaves are three times larger and remain green the year round. Its fragrant flower takes the form of a small rose. They grind the leaves into powder, which they then place in hot water — constantly kept on the fire for this purpose — and then drink that water, more for medicinal reasons than for pleasure, since its flavor is rather bitter, though it leaves one with a pleasant taste in one's mouth. Those who drink tea find that it has many beneficial effects. It is very good for those who have weak stomachs, and it is marvellously helpful to the digestion, and it is excellent for removing and preventing bad odors, so that they do not go to one's head. And in fact to drink tea after meals takes drowziness away. It is the custom therefore to drink it immediately after having eaten, particularly when one has had too much wine. The custom of drinking this *cha* is so widespread in Japan that one never enters someone's house without having a cup of it offered to him, as if out of good manners, as it is the custom to offer a glass of wine to guests in Flanders and Germany.

Carletti's descriptions are among the most lively and thorough in this early period when Japan was first becoming known to the West. He wrote of the city of Nagasaki and its homes as follows:

Francesco Carletti: *Ragionamenti . . . e d'altri Paesi*

The streets are blocked off at the end with doors, and when these latter are closed guards are posted who let no one pass unless he gives his name and says where he is going, and unless he is unmistakably recognized. Furthermore, each street has its superintendent, or shall we say Captain, who is in charge of all those living in his neighborhood, and if some crime should be committed he is made to answer for it until the wrongdoer has been taken into custody. The inhabitants themselves are called upon to prevent misdeeds in the immediate vicinity of their houses. In the city of Nagasachi these houses are all made of wood, put together with great ability, and all the materials that are used are carefully measured and prepared. A house can be set up in two days. The supporting frames are fitted into large stones at the base in the manner of foundations, half-buried in the ground, so that the wood does not come into contact with the earth and rot. Then they fit the crossbeams into the above-mentioned pillars and lay the boards which constitute the walls of the rooms and which they cover with smaller boards which are split like pine. These are nailed down. They can also serve as tiles, placed one above the other to stop up holes so that water cannot come in.

And since they are of wood and can easily catch fire, every street has a guard who throughout the night shouts, "Watch out for fire!"; for if one house catches fire, the entire city burns down, as was the case with Nagasachi. And so King Taico Sama ordered that the owner of the house that first caught fire should be crucified along with his entire family, but today this law is no longer put into effect.

In these houses of theirs they make additional rooms by means of partitions, setting up a sort of picture painted with many things and which can be opened and closed like a fan, because it is collapsible at the edges, and these not only add to comfort but are a very beautiful thing to see. And though there may be other persons in those same rooms (aside from the pleasure one takes from the painting, which depicts various types of birds and flowers and animals and abstract designs beautifully executed, with colors splashed on and lined with fine gold) one is not seen, because they are higher than the average person. They are also used to place around one's bed, so that they seem to be walls, and they are a joyous thing to see. In Japanese these paintings so to speak are called *biobus*, and they are made by uniting sheets of paper like cardboard, and then these are pasted to long lengths of wood at each end so that the center part remains empty, and then they paint them all over. They also make them of drapes of raw silk, like veils, so rich and beautifully decorated that they are often worth a hundred or two hundred *scudi* each. But the ordinary ones, which are also very beautiful, for actual use and for the everyday ornamentation of the home, cost five or ten *scudi* each.

They are also accustomed to covering their floors with certain sacks of straw two-fingers thick, four arm-lengths long and two wide covered with mats made of a grass the color of very thin straw, like that from which hats are made in our own country, and which grows in water like reeds, which in fact they may be called. The Japanese themselves call them *yo*.

And their customs are no less varied and extravagant. . . . But to mention a few of those that come to mind, what greater extravagance could there be than the way they take care of their sick, feeding them fresh salted fish with cockles and other shellfish, along with various kinds of green, bitter, and raw fruit? They never drain off blood; and so it may be said that in virtually every field they do just the very opposite of what we do.

After the persecutions against Christianity and the subsequent closing of the country not only to Catholic missionaries but also to the Portuguese and Spanish merchants, the news of the archipelago that reached Europe came almost exclusively from the Dutch. The Dutch, in fact, had received authorization to set up a base on the small island of Deshima, opposite Nagasaki; there they carried on trade and maintained a precarious point of contact with Europe up to the time the Japanese ports were reopened in the middle of the nineteenth century. Engelbert Kaempfer (1651–1716), a Dutchman who resided in Japan in 1690–92, was the author of the first "Natural, Civil, and Ecclesiastic History of Japan." Thanks to Kaempfer, the West had extensive and fairly exact information on the civilization of the archipelago during this long period of isolation. Thus, we read Kaempfer's description of the capital, Kyoto:

Engelbert Kaempfer: "Natural, Civil, and Ecclesiastical History of Japan"

In Japanese, Kio or Miaco means city. This name is given par excellence because in it lives His Holiness the Dairi, or hereditary ecclesiastic emperor, and on this basis it is considered the capital of the entire empire. It is situated in the province of Jamatto on a great plain. Its length from North to South is three-fourths of a league, and it is half-a-league wide from East to West. It is surrounded by beckoning green hills and mountains with a great many small rivers and fresh water fountains. The city is at the side of the mountain of the East, where one can see many temple-monasteries, chapels, and other religious edifices on its slopes. . . . The streets of the city are narrow but straight. Some of them head toward the South, others toward the East. If one stands at the beginning of a main street it is impossible to see the other end of it because of its extraordinary length and the crowds of people filling it. . . . Miaco is the great trading center for all the manufactures of Japan and every sort of commodity. It is the foremost commercial city in the empire. There is scarcely a house in the entire city that does not have something to buy or to sell. It is here that copper is refined, that money is coined, books are printed, and that the richest materials with gold and silver flowers are made.

These and other descriptions of the same kind represent the bulk of the information that leaked out of the archipelago up to the time of the reopening of the ports in the nineteenth century. Thereafter, the first sources of information were the travel journals and diaries of the people who visited or resided in Japan — mainly Europeans and Americans of the second half of the nineteenth century. Although such individuals tended to view matters more from the political or military viewpoints of their assigned missions, rather than from the purely cultural viewpoint, their writings did include some information on the ethnographic and artistic aspects of the country. Thus, in the account of Commodore Matthew Perry and his officers, we read the following description of the temples in the city of Simoda:

Commodore Matthew C. Perry and his Officers: *Narrative of the Expedition of an American Squadron to the China Seas and Japan, performed in the years 1852, 1853, and 1854*

There are no less than nine Buddhist temples, one large *Mia*, or Sintoo [Shinto] temple, and a great number of smaller shrines. Those devoted to the worship of Buddha have strange fanciful titles: the largest is called Rio-shen-zhi, or Buddha's obedient monastery; and there are Dai-an-zhi, or great peace monastery; the Hongaku-zhi, or source of knowledge monastery; the Too-den-zhi, or rice field monastery; the Fuku-zhen-zhi, or fountain of happiness monastery; the Chio-raku-zhi, or continual joy monastery; the Ri-gen-zhi, or source of reason monastery; and lastly, the Chio-me-zhi, or long life monastery. Twenty-five priests and a few acolytes are attached to these temples, and are supported by fees bestowed by devotees for burial services, and the various offices peculiar to Buddhism. The buildings are of wood, and although generally kept in tolerable repair, show the effects of weather upon the unpainted surface. The roofs are tiled, and project, as in the houses, beyond the walls. The posts which support the superstructure are, together with the rest of the wood work, covered with the famous Japanese lacquer. The floors, which are raised four or five feet above the ground, are neatly covered with matting. At the door of the main apartment there is a drum on the left and a bell on the right, the former of which is beaten, and the latter tingled, at the commencement of worship, to awaken the attention of the idols to the prayers of the devout. Between the door and the central shrine there are several low lecterns, or reading desks, near each of which there is conveniently placed a piece of wood carved in the shape of a fish, which is used to beat time during the chanting, which forms an important part of the religious services.

The shrine, in which are arranged the ancestral tablets, in niches, seems to be an object of particular attention, for it was kept always in perfect order, and the monuments and idols were not allowed to suffer from want of repair or of a decent regard to cleanliness. The sculpture of the various images was no better in art or more imposing in appearance than the ordinary figures of *Joss* in the Chinese temples.

On the whole, Japanese art did not particularly impress the early Western visitors, except for certain small merits they perceived in the design or execution. Thus, an early English visitor, Basil Hall Chamberlain, could write:

Basil Hall Chamberlain: *Things Japanese, Being Notes on Various Subjects Connected with Japan for the Use of Travellers and Others*

The Japanese genius touches perfection in small things. No other nation ever understood half so well how to make a cup, a tray, even a kettle a thing of beauty, how to transform a little knob of ivory into a microcosm of quaint humour, how to express a fugitive thought in half-a-dozen dashes of the pencil. The massive, the spacious, the grand, is less congenial to their mental attitude. Hence they achieve less success in architecture than in the other arts. The prospect of a Japanese city from a height is monotonous. Not a tower, not a dome, not a minaret, nothing aspiring heavenward, save in rare cases a painted pagoda half-hidden amidst the trees which it barely tops, — nothing but long, low lines of thatch and tiles, even the Buddhist temple roofs being but moderately raised above the rest, and even their curves being only quaint and graceful, nowise imposing.

The discovery of the spatial and modular values of Japanese architecture was still to come. The first European and American students of Japanese culture in modern times admired primarily the figurative arts. Travelers who went to Japan came back with their trunks full of prints, pottery, bronze pieces, and other objects of various kinds, some of them truly artistic, but some merely exotic. These first imported articles that got into circulation in the West unfortunately remained the most familiar for some time, so that the real art of the Japanese became known only sometime later. Prominent in this later appreciation was the research of such early scholars as Lafcadio Hearn, Basil Hall Chamberlain, and Ernest Fenollosa, who spent several years in Japan.

Eventually, the Japanese who came to Europe began to provide guidance to art-lovers and direct their taste to the more subtle elements of Japanese art. The French writer, Edmond de Goncourt, for instance, recognized how much his erudition on Japanese art was indebted to Hayashi, a Japanese official who had come to France. The imperial government of Japan, moreover, made a great effort to enlighten Western public opinion. For nearly twenty years, every great international exposition — Vienna in 1873, Philadelphia in 1876, Paris in 1878 — was the occasion for Japan to reveal more of its native talent. In 1900, the Japanese commission at the Paris Universal Exposition brought out a monumental history of the art of Japan, the result of long and patient research on the part of Japanese scholars. In the preface to this work, Hayashi voiced the anxieties of his countrymen who still felt that they were misunderstood and confused with their neighbors on the Asian continent. "No Japanese," he said, "is unaware of or denies the debt that the art of his country owes to China or India, but none can understand how people still fail to recognize the Japanese national originality."

Chronological Chart

DATE	JAPAN	KOREA
5000 B.C.	Jomon Culture Handworked pottery with comb and rope decorations; clay figures.	Neolithic culture. (comb pottery)
2000 B.C.	Continuation of Jomon Civilization.	Chinese scholar Ki-tze founds colony at Pyongyang (twelfth century B.C.).
1000 B.C.	Legendary foundation of the empire (660 B.C.).	Introduction of agriculture.
500 B.C.	Bronze Age.	Bronze Age. Funerary megalithism: *dolmen* tombs.
300 B.C.	Yayoi Culture Introduction of agriculture. Pottery made with a wheel.	Iron Age.
200 B.C.	Funerary megalithism; *dolmen* tombs. Spread of continental wooden architecture.	Establishment of Chinese prefecture of Lo-lang (108 B.C.).
100 B.C.	Korean embassy to Japan (33 B.C.). Building of first temple at Ise (5 B.C.).	Formation of national kingdoms: Silla (57 B.C.) Paekche (18 B.C.).

CHINA	INDIA	MIDDLE EAST	MEDITERRANEAN-WEST
Agricultural civilization in Yellow River Valley: Centers of Yang-shao painted pottery and Lung-shan black pottery (III and II millennia B.C.).	Bronze Age. Urban civilization in the Indus Valley (Mohenjo-daro and Harappa, circa 2500–1500 B.C.).	Introduction of Sothic calendar (Egypt, 4236 B.C.). Culture of painted ceramics in Mesopotamia and Persia (circa 4000 B.C.). Al Ubaid Period. Fusion of metals (Egypt circa 3700 B.C.). Sumerian invention of writing (circa 3500 B.C.). Founding of Egyptian monarchy (circa 3100 B.C.). Agriculture and irrigation in Mesopotamia and Egypt (circa 3000 B.C.). Perfecting of various systems of writing (Egyptian hieroglyphic writing, circa 2900 B.C.). Calculation of time and numerical system by the Sumerians (circa 2600 B.C.).	Aegean civilization. Cretan ceramics and geometrical decorations Cretan-Aegean writing.
Bronze Age Shang-Yin dynasty (sixteenth to eleventh centuries B.C.). Introduction of pictographic writing of the first Chinese state.	Introduction of writing. Aryan invasion.	Assyrian-Babylonian civilization. Hittite Empire (Anatolia circa 1600 B.C.). First Greek colonization in Asia Minor (circa 1200 B.C.).	Bronze Age (circa 2000 B.C.). Mycenean civilization (circa 1600 B.C.). Phoenecian civilization. Doric migration and first Greek colonization (circa 1200 B.C.).
Ideographic writing. Chou dynasty (eleventh century to 221 B.C.). Southward expansion of agricultural civilization.	Iron Age Birth of Buddha (563 B.C.).	Medes and Persians. Birth of Zoroaster (circa 660 B.C.). Founding of Byzantium (circa 660 B.C.).	Iron Age in Etruria (circa 800 B.C.): Etruscan culture. "Founding" of Rome (circa 753 B.C.). Greek colonization of Magna Graecia (750 B.C.). Greek civilization (sixth to fourth centuries B.C.).
Iron Age. Development of philosophical studies: Confucius (551–479 B.C.). Mencius (372–288 B.C.). Chuang-tzu (circa 369–286 B.C.).	Conquest of northwest India by Alexander the Great (326 B.C.). Founding of Maurya dynasty (321 B.C.).	Conquests of Alexander the Great (334–326 B.C.).	Birth of Socrates (489 B.C.). Persian wars (500–449 B.C.). Pericles. Alexander the Great (356–323 B.C.).
Legalist ideology. Founding and unification of empire (221 B.C.). Building of Great Wall.	Under imperial patronage of Asoka (273–232 B.C.), Buddhism spreads in India, Ceylon, and Indonesia. First temples and monasteries built.	Alexander's successors, Seleucids & Ptolemies, rule divided empire.	Antigonid dynasty rules Greece after Alexander. Rome gains control of Italy and defeats Carthage.
Han dynasty (206 B.C.–A.D. 220). Restoration of Confucian ideology (136 B.C.). Expansion of empire (expeditions in central Asia; colonization of part of Korea, 108 B.C.). Invention of paper (105 B.C.).	First Buddhist art in Gandhara and Mathura under Hellenistic influence. Development of Buddhist iconography. Formation of Hinduism (third century B.C.).	Hellenistic influence on culture and art of western Asia as far as India.	Greece becomes a Roman province.
Introduction of Buddhism (circa 70–50 B.C. (Mahayana).	Buddhism breaks up into Hinayana ("Small Vehicle") and Mahayana ("Great Vehicle"). Hinayana spreads through Ceylon, Indochina, and Indonesia; Mahayana through central Asia, China, and thence to Korea and Japan.	Egypt becomes a Roman province (30 B.C.).	Julius Caesar. Caesar Octavianus Augustus (31 B.C.–A.D. 14).

DATE	JAPAN	KOREA
0	Inter-tribal struggles for control; supposed submission of southern and central Japan to "emperors."	Koguryo (A.D. 37).
A.D. 200	Introduction of Chinese civilization via Korea.	Piratical raids by Japanese.
A.D. 300	Kofun Culture. Iron Age. Tumulus tombs. Funerary statuary. Shaping of state and introduction of Chinese ideographic writing. Yamato period.	Tumulus tombs. Introduction of Buddhism in Koguryo (A.D. 372) and in Paekche (A.D. 384).
A.D. 500	Introduction of Buddhism (A.D. 538 or 552). Asuka Period (A.D. 552–710).	Flowering of early Korean Buddhist art.
A.D. 600	Reign of Empress Suiko and regency of Shotoku Taishi. Patronage of Buddhism. Construction of first temples. Influx of Korean and Chinese culture in archipelago. Great reforms (Taika, A.D. 645–649). First official diplomatic missions to China.	Chinese attempts at reconquest (A.D. 612). Unification of Korea during reign of Silla (A.D. 668). Period of "great reign" of Silla (A.D. 668–935).
A.D. 700	Compilation of Taiho-Ritsuryo, the first legal code (A.D. 701). Establishment of Nara as capital (A.D. 710). Nara Period (A.D. 710–784). (First literary works: *Kojiki*. A.D. 712; *Nihon-Shoki*, A.D. 720). Imperial edict for the building of Buddhist temples in the provinces (A.D. 741). Removal of the capital from Nara to Nagaoka (A.D. 784). Final transference of the capital to Heian-kyo (Kyoto) (A.D. 794). Heian Period (A.D. 794–1185).	Buddhist art under influence of T'ang art.
A.D. 800	Introduction of printing with wooded matrixes. Spread of esoteric Buddhism (Mantrayana) (A.D. 806). Tendai and Shingon. Rise to power of Fujiwara family (A.D. 866–1160).	Continued domination of kingdom of Silla.
A.D. 900	Taira and Fugiwara families struggle with emperor. Regency of Fugiwara Michinaga (A.D. 966–1027).	Koryo dynasty (A.D. 918–1392).

CHINA	INDIA	MIDDLE EAST	MEDITERRANEAN-WEST
		Jesus Christ. Expansion of Roman Empire in Armenia and Parthia (A.D. 57–63).	Roman Empire.
Trade with Roman provinces of Asia Minor stepped up along "silk road." Alleged Roman diplomatic mission to China. Pressure exerted by nomads on Chinese borders.	Kushan empire in northern India (A.D. 125).	Dissolution of Parthian empire. Kushan Empire (A.D. 125).	
Chin dynasty (A.D. 265–420). Dynasties of central Asian origin (Wei, Liang) established in northern China; they patronize Buddhism and the setting up of monasteries.	Northern India dominated by Greek and Mongol invaders.	Advent of Sassanians in Persia (A.D. 227). Persia annexes the empire of the Kushans (A.D. 297).	Septimus Severus conquers Ecbatana in Persia (A.D. 202).
Beginnings of Buddhist art. Ku k'ai Chih (circa A.D. 344–506), painter. Northern Wei dynasty (A.D. 386–534). Six dynasties (A.D. 420–589). Cliff temples of Yun-Kang and Lung-men. Development of statuary.	Reunification of India. Gupta dynasty (A.D. 320–470). Founding of Buddhist university of Nalanda. Flourishing of literature and arts. Invasion of northern India by Huns (A.D. 494).	Constantinople as capital of the Roman Empire (A.D. 330). Invasion of Persia by Huns (A.D. 429).	The Huns' first invasion of the Roman Empire (A.D. 395). Ravenna as capital of the Roman Empire in West (A.D. 402). Sack of Rome by Alaric (A.D. 410). Fall of the Roman Empire of the West (A.D. 476).
Legendary arrival from India of Bodhidharma (A.D. 520), patriarch of Ch'an Buddhism. Sui dynasty (A.D. 581–618).	India invaded and shattered by Huns from north.	Founding of the Turkish Empire (A.D. 552). Mohammed (A.D. 570–632).	Reign of the Longobards (A.D. 568).
Tang dynasty (A.D. 618–907). Initial conquests of Korea and Turkestan (A.D. 639). Intensification of trade relations with western Asia. Cosmopolitanism of Chinese life and culture. Great flourishing of literature and art.	Harsha, last native Indian king, reconquers much of Gupta empire and rules till A.D. 647.	Beginning of the Hegira (July 15, 622). Arab conquests of Syria (A.D. 636). The Sassanian King Yazdgard III asks China in vain for help against the Arabs (A.D. 638), who complete the conquest of Persia in A.D. 651. Writing of the Koran (A.D. 653). Foundation of Omayyad caliphate (A.D. 660).	Merovingians extend rule of Franks through much of Western Europe.
Astronomy and mathematics flourish. T'ang dynasty threatened by various tribes and generals.	India divided into small principalities. First Moslem invaders in A.D. 712; expelled by Indians by about A.D. 750.	Ommiad Caliphate, based in Damascus, extends power in Middle East and to West. Founding of Baghdad (A.D. 762). Arab numerical system (A.D. 773).	Arab conquest of Spain (A.D. 711). Defeat of Arabs at Poitiers (A.D. 732). Omayyad caliphate of Cordoba (A.D. 756). Charlemagne (A.D. 768–814).
China split by various local military leaders. Persecution of Buddhism (A.D. 845).	India weak and divided by dynastic rivalries.	Spreading and flourishing of Moslem power and culture.	Byzantium reestablishes its dominion over southern Italy (A.D. 880–892).
Period of Five Dynasties and Ten States.	Turkish invasions. Development of Tantrist Buddhism (Mantrayana and Vajsarayama).		Otto the Great extends order across Europe.
Sung dynasty established (A.D. 960–1279).	Conquest of Mahmud in Punjab.	Establishment of Cairo as Fatimid capital (A.D. 973). Avicenna (circa A.D. 980–1037). Seljuk conquests.	Establishment of Holy Roman Empire (A.D. 962).

DATE	JAPAN	KOREA
A.D. 1000	Golden age of literature (*Genji Monogatari*).	
		Production of Celadon-type ceramics.
A.D. 1100	Increased weakening of central power. Civil disorders. Progressive decline of Fujiwara authority. Struggles between Taira and Minamoto families (A.D. 1155–1185). Battle of Dannoura (A.D. 1185). Minamoto Yoritome as Shogun (Generalissimo) sets up military government at Kamakura (1192). Kamakura period (A.D. 1185–1333). Introduction of Ch'an (Zen) Buddhism from China (A.D. 1191).	
A.D. 1200		Invasions by the Mongols (A.D. 1231–1235). First use of movable characters in metal for printing (A.D. 1234). Surrender of Koryo dynasty to the Yuans (A.D. 1239).
	Attempts at invasion by the Mongols (A.D. 1274–1281).	
A.D. 1300	Restoration of imperial power under Go-Daigo (A.D. 1333). Ashikaga Takauji reestablishes the shogunate at Kyoto (A.D. 1336). Trade with China. Muromachi or Ashikaga period (A.D. 1336–1602).	Restoration of the national monarchy. Choson or Yi Period (A.D. 1392–1910). Abolition of Buddhism as state religion and proclamation of Confucianism as official doctrine.
A.D. 1400	Renewed relations with China (A.D. 1401). The War of Onin (A.D. 1467): struggle between branches of the Ashikaga family.	Setting up of state printing office (A.D. 1403) with the use of movable characters.
A.D. 1500	Landing of first Portuguese (A.D. 1542 or 1543) and introduction of firearms. Beginning of Christian preaching with Francesco Saverio (A.D. 1549). Imperial legation sent to Pope Gregory XIII (A.D. 1582–1603). Expedition of Hideyoshi to Korean peninsula (A.D. 1592–1598). First persecutions of Christianity (A.D. 1597).	Japanese attempts at conquest (A.D. 1592–1598). Arrival of Jesuit missionary Gregorio Cespedes (A.D. 1594) and beginning of Christian preaching.

CHINA	INDIA	MIDDLE EAST	MEDITERRANEAN-WEST
Sung rulers extend peace and prosperity to much of China.	Mahmud extends Moslem power in northern India. Cholas dynasty dominates southern India.	Protectorate over the Abbasid caliphate of Baghdad (A.D. 1055). Taking of Jerusalem by Crusaders (A.D. 1090).	Fall of Cordoba caliphate (A.D. 1031). First Crusade.
Sung rulers maintain period of economic and intellectual distinction. Neo-Confucianism of Chu-hsi (A.D. 1130–1200).	Invasion and conquest of Muhammad of Ghor. Persecution of Buddhism in Magadha (A.D. 1195).	Averroes (A.D. 1126–1198). Egypt and Syria under Saladin (A.D. 1171–1174).	Concordat of Worms (A.D. 1122). Second and Third Crusades. Kingdom of Sicily (A.D. 1127).
Mongol occupation of northern China. Marco Polo's arrival in China (A.D. 1271). Mongol dynasty of the Yuans (A.D. 1279–1368) (attempts to conquer Japan). Kublai Kahn on Chinese throne (A.D. 1280).	Successors of Muhammad of Ghor established Sultanate of Delhi (A.D. 1206–1526). Sultanate of Delhi (A.D. 1206–1526).	Taking of Constantinople by Fourth Crusade (A.D. 1204). Turkish-Mongolian unification of Genghis Kahn (A.D. 1206). Conquest of Persia by Mongols (A.D. 1220–1223). Taking of Jerusalem by the Turks (A.D. 1244). Dynasty of Mamelukes in Egypt (A.D. 1250–1517).	Fourth Crusade. Reconquest of part of Spain from Moslems. Emperor Frederick II ("Marvel of the World"). The Magna Carta (A.D. 1215).
Propagation of Christianity: Giovanni da Monte Cervine and Odorico do Pordenone arrive in China. Marignolli Papal legation (A.D. 1342–1345). Ming dynasty (A.D. 1368–1644). Defeat of the Mongols (A.D. 1388).	Mongol invasion (A.D. 1303). Tamerlane (Timur) conquers the Sultanate of Delhi (A.D. 1399).	Conquests of Tamerlane (A.D. 1365). Emir Timur ascends throne of Samarkand (A.D. 1369).	Beginning of Hundred Years' War (A.D. 1339). Grand Papal diplomatic delegation sent to China (A.D. 1370). Great Schism in West (A.D. 1378)
Expansion on Indochinese peninsula and annexation of Vietnam (A.D. 1406). Anti-Buddhist and anti-Taoist persecutions (A.D. 1487).	Disorder follows Tamurlane's invasion. India divided by rival dynasties and tribes.	Fall of the Byzantine Empire to the Ottoman conquest (A.D. 1453).	Gutenberg's press (A.D. 1450). Discovery of America (A.D. 1492). Vasco de Gama's voyage (A.D. 1497–1500).
Anti Buddhist persecutions (A.D. 1521–1566). Imperial order to destroy all Buddhist images in Peking (A.D. 1556). Arrival of Matteo Ricci (A.D. 1552), followed by Dominican Jasparo la Cruz (A.D. 1554). Propagation of Catholic faith among the nobility.	Albuquerque and first Portuguese possession (A.D. 1503). Founding of Bombay by Portuguese (A.D. 1530). Invasion of Baber and beginning of Mogul dynasty (A.D. 1526–1761).	Ottoman conquest of Egypt (A.D. 1517). Suleiman the Magnificent (A.D. 1520–1566) extends Ottoman power into Europe and besieges Vienna.	Albuquerque and the shaping of Portuguese Empire (A.D. 1503). Magellan's voyage (A.D. 1519). Landing of first Spaniards in Philippines (A.D. 1521). Organization of Society of Jesus (A.D. 1539). Beginning of Spanish occupation of Philippines (A.D. 1565).

DATE	JAPAN	KOREA
A.D. 1600	Edo, or Tokugawa, Period (A.D. 1602–1867). Beginning of trade with Dutch East India Company (A.D. 1609). Expulsion of Portuguese merchants and closing of country (A.D. 1636–1639). Dutch concession in Deshima (A.D. 1641).	Manchu invasions (A.D. 1627–1636) Vassalage to China (A.D. 1637).
A.D. 1700	Introduction of European medical science (A.D. 1774).	Anti-Christian persecutions.
A.D. 1800	Arrival of Commodore Perry (USA) and Admiral Potiantin (Russia) to negotiate the reopening of the ports. End of isolation and reopening of the nation to outside world (A.D. 1853–1858). Meiji restoration (A.D. 1868).	

CHINA	INDIA	MIDDLE EAST	MEDITERRANEAN-WEST
Translation of Aesop's Fables into Chinese (A.D. 1625).	Founding of British and Dutch East India companies (A.D. 1601–1602). Founding of Dutch West India Company (A.D. 1621).	Ottomans conclude peace treaty with Persia. Violence and disorder mark Ottoman Empire.	Beginning of Dutch domination in Indonesia (A.D. 1605). Setting up of French East India Company (A.D. 1664).
Ching dynasty (A.D. 1644–1912).			Siege of Vienna by the Turks (A.D. 1683). Peace of Karlowitz and withdrawal of Ottoman empire (A.D. 1699).
Jesuit atlas of Father Regis (A.D. 1711). Settlement of Sino-Russian borders (A.D. 1727): Jesuit painters Attiret and Castiglione at the imperial court (A.D. 1741). First English diplomatic missions (A.D. 1793, 1816). Opening of port of Canton to traffic with foreign countries (A.D. 1793).	British East India Company obtains trading concession from Mogul Empire (A.D. 1716). British and French war for control of India; French abandon struggle (A.D. 1754). British Governor Generalship in India (A.D. 1774).	Napoleon's campaign in Egypt (A.D. 1798–1799). First indications of Arab revival.	Peace of Utrecht (A.D. 1713). Seven Years' War (A.D. 1756–1763). American Revolution. French Revolution.
First Protestant missions (1807). Opium War (A.D. 1839–1842). Concession of Hong Kong to England (A.D. 1842). T'ai P'ing revolution (A.D. 1851–1864)	Sepoy revolt and reorganization of India (A.D. 1857–1858).	Ottoman Empire gradually losing power and territories.	Napoleon Bonaparte Russian mission to Japan (A.D. 1804–1805). United States and Russia ask reopening of Japanese ports (A.D. 1853). Franco-British war against China (A.D. 1857–1860). French occupation of Indochina (A.D. 1859–1867).

Recommended Reading

In the years following the reopening of Japan a great many Westerners were drawn to the country. Their published responses to the culture they found there are included in the list that follows, together with more recent books on Japanese life, art, history, and thought. The original studies remain the classic ones, but interest in Japanese culture continues to grow, not least because of Japan's present-day importance in world affairs, and Japanese writers have now produced studies of their own culture which are of interest to American and European readers.

In the selection of books which follows, emphasis has been placed on those which are readily accessible to the general reader, not only in terms of their price, but because of their recent editions and their general tone of exposition.

Alex, William: *Japanese Architecture* (Braziller, 1963)

Binyon, Lawrence: *Painting in the Far East* (Dover, 1960)

Chamberlain, Basil Hall: *Japanese Things* (Tuttle, 1970)

Cram, Ralph Adams: *Impressions of Japanese Architecture and the Allied Arts* (Dover, 1966)

Dunn, Charles: *Everyday Life in Traditional Japan* (Putnam, 1969)

Fenollosa, Ernest F.: *Epochs of Chinese and Japanese Art* (Dover, 1963)

Hearn, Lafcadio: *Japan: An Interpretation* (Tuttle, 1955)

Ishimoto, Tatsuo: *Art of the Japanese Garden* (Crown, 1958)

Johnson, Erwin, ed.: *Peoples and Cultures of Japan* (Doubleday Anchor, 1970)

Keene, Donald, ed.: *Anthology of Japanese Literature: from the Earliest Era to Mid-Nineteenth Century* (in translation) (Grove, 1956)

Kidder, J. Edward, Jr.: *Japan before Buddhism* (Praeger, 1966)

Leonard, Jonathan N.: *Early Japan* (Time-Life, 1970)

Masuda, Tomoya: *Living Architecture: Japanese* (Grosset & Dunlap, 1971)

Morris, Ivan: *The World of the Shining Prince* (Penguin, 1969)

Morse, Edward S.: *Japanese Homes and Their Surroundings* (Dover, 1961)

Munsterberg, Hugo: *The Arts of Japan:* An Illustrated History (Tuttle, 1956)

Okakura, Kakuzo: *The Book of Tea* (Tuttle)

Paine, Robert T. and Soper, Alexander: *The Art and Architecture of Japan* (Penguin, 1955)

Reischauer, Edwin O.: *Japan: Past and Present*, fourth edn. (Knopf, 1970)

Rudofsky, Bernard: *The Kimono Mind* (Doubleday, 1965)

Sansom, George B.: *Japan: A Short Cultural History*, revised (Appleton, 1962)

Statler, Oliver: *Japanese Inn* (Random, 1961)

Suzuki, Daisetz T.: *Zen and Japanese Culture* (Princeton University Press 1959)
Zen Buddhism, Selected Writings of D. T. Suzuki, ed. by William Barrett (Doubleday Anchor, 1956)

Swann, Peter C.: *The Art of China, Korea, and Japan* (Praeger, 1963)
The Art of Japan (Crown, 1966)

Warner, Langdon: *The Enduring Art of Japan* (Grove, 1958)

Short of a visit to Japan, the best way to experience that nation's culture is to visit a museum display of Japanese art and artifacts. North America is fortunate in having considerable collections of Japanese art — indeed, the finest and most extensive outside of Japan itself. Some of it is on permanent display, some appears in special or occasional exhibits; some are full survey collections of Japanese culture, some are merely individual pieces in general collections of Far Eastern art; some are of interest primarily to students of Japanese culture, while some will attract people with special interests such as ceramics or prints. The list below includes all such collections — most of them open, within certain restrictions, to the general public — that offer people everywhere a chance to enjoy some acquaintance with the productions of this exceptional civilization.

Recommended Viewing

Arizona: Tucson: University of Arizona Art Gallery
California: La Jolla Art Center
   *Los Angeles County Museum
   Oakland Art Museum
   *San Francisco: Center of Asian Art and Culture (Brundage and deYoung Collections)
   Santa Barbara Museum of Art
   Stanford: University Art Gallery
Colorado: Denver Art Museum
Connecticut: New Haven: Yale University Art Gallery
District of Columbia: *Washington: Freer Gallery of Art
Hawaii: *Honolulu Academy of Arts
Illinois: *Chicago: The Art Institute
Indiana: Bloomington: Indiana University Museum of Art
   Indianapolis Museum of Art
Iowa: Davenport: Municipal Art Gallery and Public Museum
Maryland: Baltimore: The Walters Art Gallery
Massachusetts: *Boston: Museum of Fine Arts
   Cambridge: *Harvard University, Fogg Art Museum
   Salem: Peabody Museum
   *Worcester Art Museum
Michigan: *Detroit Institute of Art
Minnesota: Minneapolis Institute of Arts
Missouri: Kansas City: *Nelson Gallery–Atkins Museum
   St. Louis: City Art Museum
New York: New York City: Asia House Gallery (occasional)
   *Brooklyn Museum (and adjacent Botanical Gardens with replicas of Japanese gardens)
   *Japan House Gallery
   *Metropolitan Museum of Art (to be displayed in 1974)
   Museum of Modern Art (contemporary art)
   New York Public Library (prints)
Ohio: Cincinnati Art Museum
   *Cleveland Museum of Art
   Dayton Art Institute
Oregon: Eugene: University of Oregon Museum of Art
   Portland Art Museum
Pennsylvania: *Philadelphia Museum of Art
Washington: *Seattle Art Museum
Wisconsin: Madison: University of Wisconsin, The Wisconsin Union
CANADA: Montreal Museum of Fine Arts
   *Toronto: The Royal Ontario Museum

*especially fine collections

Index

(*Numbers in italics refer to pages of illustration captions*)